Defence of the Seven Sacraments

New Millennium Edition

HENRY VIII
KING OF ENGLAND, DEFENDER OF THE FAITH

EDITED AND SUPPLEMENTED BY RAYMOND DE SOUZA

SAINT GABRIEL COMMUNICATIONS INTERNATIONAL
UNITED STATES – AUSTRALIA – SOUTH AFRICA

© Copyright 2020
Saint Gabriel Communications International
All rights reserved.

Defence of the Seven Sacraments. New Millennium Edition. All rights reserved. Printed in Australia. Graphic design by Dominic de Souza. No part of this new translation and original supplements may be used or reproduced in any manner whatsoever without written permission except in the case of brief quotations embodied in critical articles or reviews. For information please address the Editor.

Saint Gabriel Communications International
PO Box 1393 Conyngham PA 18219-1393
UNITED STATES OF AMERICA
www.SaintGabriel-International.com

FOR MORE COPIES, CONTACT

Parousia Media (Australian Distributor)
PO Box 59, Galston NSW 2159 Australia
(02) 9651-0375

www.parousiamedia.com | office@parousiamedia.com

Defence of the Seven Sacraments

The Royal Book of Catholic Apologetics

Authored by a King

Assisted by a Saint

Acclaimed by a Pope

Contents

Page

Foreword 6

Dedication 9

From the Editor 11

Warning 14

Preface by Cardinal Gibbons 17

Letter of Henry VIII to Pope Leo X 21

Letter of Leo X to Henry VIII 25

Henry VIII's Epistle Dedicatory 28

Leo X's Papal Bull 30

Henry VIII's Defence of the Seven Sacraments

Note from the Author 35

To the Reader 37

Chapter I - Of Indulgences 41

Chapter II – Of the Pope's Authority 46

Chapter III - The Defence of the Seven Sacraments 51

Chapter IV - The Sacrament of the Altar 53

The Sacrament of the Eucharist under one form only administered to the laity 56

About Transubstantiation 62

The Mass is a Good Work 74

The Sacrifice of the Mass 85

Chapter V - Of Baptism 97

The Laws of Rulers are to be obeyed 106

Chapter VI – Of the Sacrament of Penance 110

Chapter VII - Of Contrition 112

Chapter VIII – Of Confession 116

Chapter IX – Of Satisfaction 125

Chapter X – of Confirmation 130

Chapter XI – Of the Sacrament of Marriage 136

Chapter XII - Of the Sacrament of Order 150

Chapter XIII - Of the Sacrament of Extreme Unction 168

Postface 178

To our fellow Catholics 186

To our separated Brethren 200

On the Dictatorship of Relativism 205

Apostolic letter *Amantissima voluntatis* 211

Prayers for England 215

Saint Thomas More, Patron of Statesmen 219

In Memoriam 223

A vision of the Future 227

Saint Gabriel Communications 230

Foreword

"A spectre haunts Europe - the spectre of Communism. The Powers of old Europe entered into a holy alliance to exorcise this spectre."

Thus read the defiant opening line of the Communist Manifesto, 1848. In spite of all the death and destruction it caused, Communism failed to conquer Europe.

Today, Europe and the West are being conquered by another haunting spectre: *De-Christianisation*. A major difference: the Powers of Europe have NOT entered into a holy alliance to exorcise the new spectre.

Instead, they co-operate with it - albeit in different ways.

Europe, cradle of Christendom, is destroying its own civilisation. National and regional traditions succumb to a revolution that degrades local cultures down to the same level of insipidness. Political systems obliterate countries' sovereignties and people's natural rights.

Christianity is at its lowest; if, by the end of this century, most European cathedrals have not been turned into museums, theatres or mosques, it will be a miracle. Massive immigration from non-

Christian countries has caused severe social problems - to put it rather mildly.

Moral decadence brought about by drugs, pornography, unbridled promiscuity, abortion and homosexuality wrecks the mother-cell of society - the family. A hedonistic, contraceptive mentality prevents normal population growth. Result: decadence en route to extinction.

Nations without children are nations without future.

Pius XII denounced *"the threat that hangs over humanity: economy without God, law without God, politics without God."*

But the destructive process of de-Christianisation precedes Communism by centuries. It has been spreading since the 16th century, when doctrinal and moral relativism fragmented Christianity and inspired an endless series of contradictory religious denominations, all claiming to be 'Bible-based'.

If the Christian West is to survive both as Christian and as Western, the re-unification of Christians is a necessary, preliminary step.

The publication of *"Defence of the Seven Sacraments"* is aimed to make a contribution to this so desirable an end: **unity in Truth.**

Raymond de Souza

Dedication

Dieu et mon Roi – Béni soit qui bien y pense

To Her Majesty Elizabeth the Second, by the Grace of God of the United Kingdom of Great Britain and Northern Ireland, Australia, Canada, New Zealand and her other Realms and Territories Queen; Head of the Commonwealth, and to her successors to the throne according to Law, this New Millennium edition of 'Defence of the Seven Sacraments' by King Henry VIII is devotedly dedicated.

This edition is a respectful and fraternal reminder of that peaceful unity in *'One Lord, one Faith, one Baptism'* (Eph. 4:5) which Merry England – the 'Dowry of the Virgin Mary' – shared with the Apostolic See of Rome for nearly one thousand years, especially in the glorious days of the sweet springtime of our Faith, when the philosophy of the Gospel governed the States in mediaeval Christendom.

May Our Lady of Walsingham prayerfully intercede for Her Majesty, the Royal family and the whole Anglican, Congregational, Episcopalian, Methodist and all communities that issued from England; so that, by acknowledging the fullness of the Apostolic teaching on the seven Sacraments - so fiercely defended by King Henry VIII - they may help restore the unity of all the baptised in the Body of Christ, for the greater glory of God, salvation of souls, as well as peace and prosperity for all Christian nations.

From Her Majesty's loyal subject,

Raymond Joseph de Souza

Brazilian by birth, Catholic by grace, Australian by choice.

On the second day of June in the year of Our Lord Jesus Christ of two thousand and seven, the fifty-fourth anniversary of Her Majesty's Coronation.

"Ubi Ecclesia ibi Christus, ubi Petrus ibi Ecclesia"

From the Editor

The wish to publish a revised, New Millennium Edition of Henry VIII's work 'Defence of the Seven Sacraments' had its origin after the celebration organised in New Zealand on the occasion of Her Majesty's 40th anniversary of accession to the throne.

Led by a group of young pipers, members and supporters of the Monarchy Institute of New Zealand (Te Ropu Arikitanga o Aotearoa) paraded down Wellington's major artery, Lambton Quay, heading towards Parliament grounds.

There, members of both Houses of Parliament, including Ministers of the Crown, were present to receive the parade. It was an unpretentious, yet meaningful celebration of a great event.

In that evening's party, the champagne toast was raised to Her Majesty, Elizabeth II, *Dei Gratia Britanniarum Regnorumque Suorum Ceterorum Regina, Consortionis Populorum Princeps*. All wished her health, happiness and long to reign over us.

During the conversations, various issues related to the Monarchy were raised and amicably discussed by Her Majesty's loyal subjects.

The topics were as timely as they were varied: the Monarchy-Republic debate; New Zealand's absent Monarch; the controversies raised by the media regarding the young royals' lifestyles; the exclusion of Roman Catholics from the English Royal throne.

Historical considerations and individual views were exchanged on the aforesaid exclusion, as well as the appropriateness of a new Act of Parliament in Britain to have it removed. This was not surprising, since all present were Roman Catholics themselves. Such an Act would restore the rights of Catholics in the British Monarchy.

The book written by Henry VIII was then mentioned as the greatest contribution to the defence of the Catholic Faith ever made by an English King.

The idea of a new edition emerged quite naturally, as a fraternal reminder to our separated brethren of the original meaning and purpose of the title *'Fidei Defensor'*.

The title was first conferred by Pope Leo X on Henry VIII (Oct. 11, 1521) as a reward for the king's work titled *Assertio septem sacramentorum adversus Martinum Lutherum* ("Defence of the Seven Sacraments Against Martin Luther").

History tells us that Henry later denied a key belief he had so valiantly defended: the Primacy of the Bishop of Rome over the Universal Church. Today, the coronation oath refers to the defence of the Protestant Faith.

As a cultured lay scholar, Henry VIII wrote the *Assertio septem sacramentorum* in Latin. The most recent English version of his work was published precisely one hundred years ago, in 1907, by Rev. Louis O'Donovan, S.T.L. (*Nihil Obstat* by Remy Lafont, Censor Librorum and *Imprimatur* by John M, Farley, Archbishop of New York, on 27 December 1907).

That edition was beautifully prefaced by His Eminence James Cardinal Gibbons, the great Archbishop of Baltimore.

Rev. O'Donovan's scholarly English translation skilfully reflected the richness of the Latin style used by Henry VIII by retaining the long sentences supplemented with glosses and parenthetical insertions, which was certainly suitable to English-speaking readers one hundred years ago, but could render the translation much too literal and somewhat difficult to follow by a contemporary English-speaking reader not used to long sentences.

We felt that a simple repetition of that style would not be appropriate to today's readers. On the other hand, to bring the text completely up to date would necessarily render King Henry's style unrecognisable.

In medio stat virtus. We opted for a middle course. Always thoroughly faithful to the thoughts and words of the royal author, as well as to his uniquely colourful style, our task was to simplify the syntax and break up the long paragraphs into shorter sentences. In this manner the book would be more easily understood and appreciated by the contemporary English-speaking reader.

It was a challenge we joyfully accepted. We hope we have succeeded in our task. We trust that this limited simplification will retain much of Henry VIII's style, manner and characteristic ardour.

In order to highlight his orthodoxy, we have added over one hundred quotations from the *Compendium of the Catholic Catechism*, which was given by Pope Benedict XVI to the Universal Church in 2005.

By reading the footnotes along with the text, the reader may be pleasantly surprised to realise how faithful Henry VIII was to the perennial teachings of the Magisterium of the Church.

Last but not least, it is an undeniable fact that the Episcopal consecration of women in the Anglican Church and that of a practicing homosexual in the Episcopalian church in America, besides doing a great disservice to the cause of authentic Christian unity, have torn those communities apart, much like the Temple veil on the day of Christ's death.

As a result, a large number of the faithful in those communities are gradually coming to realise that such consecrations demonstrably do not reflect the Mind of Christ. Reportedly, a great many are considering ways to come home to Rome.

We hope that the attentive reading of the *Assertio Septem Sacramentorum* will be helpful to clarify the issues and promote the authentic reunification of all baptised Christians.

We respectfully ask you, dear reader, to join us in prayer so that this final reunification may soon become a reality – especially in our days when the enemies of the Cross of Christ make great strides within the once Christian Europe and the Western world.

Raymond J de Souza – Editor

My heartfelt thanks to my beloved wife, Theresa, for her continued support and encouragement, as well as to my son Dominic and my good friend Kenneth Skuba, for the indefatigable and skilled assistance they provided in the work of editing and proof-reading this historical book.

Scriptural quotations taken from the Douay-Rheims version.
Footnotes taken from the Compendium of the Catechism of the Catholic Church.

Warning

There are certain kinds of people who are advised not to read this book.

It was not written for the lukewarm, the apathetic or the mediocre. Unconcerned as they are about objective truth and reality, they systematically avoid controversy at all costs and view courageous effort and risk as the ultimate evil, which they are never prepared to face. They vainly try to adjust their views to please everyone, even at the risk of displeasing God Himself.

It was not written for the worshippers of relativistic ecumenism. Indifferent to the glory of God and salvation of souls, they imagine that any religious denomination, large or small, old or new, will always be favourably acknowledged before the throne of Christ as His Church and Bride. To them, it matters little if such churches were established according to individual whims and preferences, objections, hair-splitting Bible interpretations or subjective moral or doctrinal choices.

Above all, it was not written for the agnostics and relativists, who do not *recognise anything as absolute and leave as the ultimate measure only the measure of each one and his desires;** who accept religion only as a private matter, as long as it does not upset their petty comforts and lifestyles.

Such people are unable to appreciate the fact that a counterfeit understanding of ecumenism, imbued with irenic relativism, has infiltrated the minds of a very large number of baptised Christians today, including Church authorities. Ignoring as it does the objective Revelation handed down by the Apostles, such a mental attitude assumes that any creed or code of ethics is an acceptable expression of the Christian Faith, as long as it is regarded as 'sincere' and upsets no one; for such men, sincerity in belief is sufficient proof of legitimacy and truthfulness.

They overlook the fact that only the unsullied, objective truth shall set them genuinely free, and lead them to authentic happiness in this life and in the hereafter.

It could be said that Henry VIII wrote this book for men of *mature faith, who do not follow fashions and the latest novelty, but rather are profoundly rooted in friendship with Christ.**

Such men believe in the entire divine Revelation given to the Apostles by Jesus Christ, who founded one Church, not many, His only Bride against whom the gates of hell shall never prevail.

That same Jesus Christ sent the Holy Spirit, Who, in turn, inspired some of the Church's first Bishops to write the New Testament and later guided Her to separate the inspired Books from the apocrypha.

The Spirit of God is He Who guides the Church, whose Magisterium is the sole authentic interpreter of Sacred Scripture and the Apostolic Tradition.

The Church founded by Jesus Christ administers the seven Sacraments that He instituted as the ordinary means to receive divine grace unto eternal salvation.

It could also be said that when Henry VIII wrote 'Defence of the Seven Sacraments', he realised that *Catholics could not remain immature in the faith, in a state of inferiority, as they run the risk of being tossed about and carried here and there by any doctrinal wind. He felt that a clear faith, according to the creed of the Church, was needed.**

In short, it was primarily to safeguard the integrity of the true Faith, delivered to the Apostles, and to call all men to salvation in the Church founded by Jesus Christ, that the King of England and France, and Lord of Ireland, wrote this book.

We pray, dear Reader, that you will be among those who accept or will accept the Faith whose integrity Henry VIII endeavoured to protect and safeguard in writing the *'Assertio septem sacramentorum adversus Martinum Lutherum'* - Defence of the Seven Sacraments Against Martin Luther.

- *Joseph Cardinal Ratzinger, homily at the Conclave that elected him Pope.*

Preface

By His Eminence James Cardinal Gibbons, Archbishop of Baltimore, for the 1907 edition of Henry VIII's Defence of the Seven Sacraments.

The *"Assertio Septem Sacramentorum"*, or "Defence of the Seven Sacraments," by Henry VIII, King of England and 'Defender of the Faith,' is a rare, royal, Catholic book.

It is rare, inasmuch as it has probably been printed but twice in nearly 200 years. It is a royal book, by reason of its kingly author. It is Catholic, because no Catholic could write a more orthodox treatise on the subjects here explained by King Henry VIII.

Yet he expounds such crucial dogmas as the primacy of the Bishop of Rome, indulgences, the mystery of the Real Presence and the Mass, the Sacrament of Confession, divorce, etc. And all this he has unfolded in as Catholic a manner as St. Thomas, or St. Francis de Sales, or St. Alphonsus Liguori could have done.

But besides the matter of the treatise, the period also when it was composed - a most interesting, even if saddening, epoch in the history of the Church - makes the work most valuable. For just at that date -1521- the cauldron of the so-called Reformation was boiling furiously in Germany.

But in England, Henry boasted that its horrors had not yet begun, and, moreover, he posed as the champion of the Church, to see that Luther's novelties should not appear there. And this freedom from the "reform" he was ready to maintain by his sword if later need be, but at any rate now.

And Henry was quite well equipped for his self-assumed task, having improved his natural talents by an education intended to prepare him to be Archbishop of Canterbury. Little wonder then that he should have written such a book as the "Defence of the Seven Sacraments," which, after all, is only a simple, plain, yet strong explanation of the Church's teachings on some of her most vital points.

In act the first, Henry is a young, brilliant, powerful, Catholic king with the best of Catholic women for his queen, ruling in peace over Catholic, Merry England.

In act the second, he has become the adulterer, the divorcé, the wife-killer, and with it all, and because of it all, he has become a schismatic, the head of a schism, dragging his subjects away from Catholic unity, and making them acknowledge himself not only their earthly king, but their spiritual head.

And yet it was only a few years before that Henry had written this book, for which Pope Leo X had given him the title "Defender of the Faith," a title prized and used by every subsequent sovereign of England.

This book, therefore, from so many points of view, is one that must be of interest to every student of either English history or of the history of religion in general. [It] should appeal to and reach many readers, not only in this country but especially in England.

[It] brings before you King Henry's own words, showing that he who later became the first head of the Protestant Church in England was, together with all the people of England in those olden days, truly Catholic and violently opposed to Luther and his destructive and murderous reform.

I hope, therefore, that the work may be widely and carefully read, especially in this country, but indeed also in England, the land of its birth.

James Card. Gibbons, Archbishop of Baltimore, U.S.A.
[Excerpts]

WALSINGHAM ABBEY.

Henry VIII's Letter to Pope Leo X on the subject of his book "Assertio Septem Sacramentorum"

ost Holy Father:

No duty is more incumbent on a Catholic sovereign than to preserve and increase the Christian faith and religion and the proofs thereof, and to transmit them preserved thus inviolate to posterity, by his example in preventing them from being destroyed by any assailant of the Faith or in any wise impaired.

So, when we learned that the pest of Martin Luther's heresy had appeared in Germany and was raging everywhere, without let or hindrance, to such an extent that many, infected with its poison, were falling away, especially those whose furious hatred rather than their zeal for Christian Truth had prepared them to believe all its subtleties and lies; we were so deeply grieved at this heinous crime of the German nation (for whom we have no light regard), and for the sake of the Holy Apostolic See, that we bent all our thoughts and energies on uprooting in every possible way, this cockle, this heresy from the Lord's flock.

When we perceived that this deadly venom had advanced so far and had seized upon the weak and ill-disposed minds of so many, that it could not easily be overcome by a single effort, we deemed that nothing could be more efficient in destroying the contagion than to declare these errors worthy of condemnation, after they had been examined by a convocation of learned and scholarly men from all parts of our realm.

This course of action we likewise recommended to a number of others. In the first place, we earnestly entreated His Imperial Majesty, through our fraternal love for him, and all the electoral princes, to bethink them of their Christian duty and their lofty station and to destroy this pernicious man, together with his scandalous and heretical publications, after his refusal to return to God.

But convinced that, in our ardour for the welfare of Christendom, in our zeal for the Catholic Faith and our devotion to the Apostolic See, we had not yet done enough, we determined to show by our own writings our attitude towards Luther and our opinion of his vile books; to manifest more openly to all the world that we shall ever defend and uphold the Holy Roman Church, not only by force of arms but by the resources of our intelligence and our services as a Christian.

For this reason we have thought that this first attempt of our modest ability and learning could not be more worthily dedicated than to your Holiness, both as a token of our filial reverence and an acknowledgment of your careful solicitude for the weal of Christendom.

We feel assured that our first fruits will be enhanced in value if it be approved by the wholesome judgment of your Blessedness. May you live long and happily!

From our Royal Palace at Greenwich, the twenty-first day of May, 1521.

Your Holiness' most devoted and humble son, Henry, by the grace of God King of England and France, and Lord of Ireland.

Letter from Leo X to Henry VIII Respecting the "Defence of the Seven Sacraments" In Acknowledgment of the Book Written by the King against Luther

o Our Most Christian Son in Christ, Henry, King of England, Illustrious Defender of the Faith.

Most dear Son in Christ, Health and Apostolic Benediction:

Some days ago, when the envoy of Your Serenity, Our beloved Son, John Clark, Dean of the Chapel Royal, publicly in Consistory presented us the book which Your Serenity has published against the impious teachings and sect of Martin Luther, and, in a brilliant address, exceedingly appropriate to the occasion, declared, in the presence of a number of Prelates of the Roman Court, your readiness to aid Us and the Holy See with sword and pen, our soul was filled with joy.

Not We alone, but all Our venerable brethren rejoiced, as though deeming that Luther's impiety had, not without the divine permission, assailed the Church of Christ, so that to Her greater glory She might be fortunate enough to find such a Champion and Defender.

Hence We have resolved, and all agree in Our decision, that your exceptional virtue and piety should be made memorable by some mark of Our love and appreciation.

For if it has often been, most dear Son, a source of honour to great Monarchs to take up arms to safeguard the liberty and tranquillity of the Holy Apostolic See, how much more glory and reverence should accrue from employing the weapons of the Spirit of God and of heavenly science to remove from the Faith of Christ so great a stain, and to preserve inviolate those sacraments by which the salvation of souls is secured.

These two functions, which hitherto We have always found separate, have been united in you alone, a mighty Sovereign, in a most eminent degree; for you have both vindicated the liberty of the Church with your arms, and you have evinced your desire to fortify the Christian Faith against impious heresy by the treasures of your piety and learning.

The one is an evidence of invincible and lofty courage, the other of a spirit and sense of religion tender, devout, and orthodox.

In what words, then, or by what manner of eulogy shall we praise this piety, this plenitude of doctrine, overflowing as though from a celestial fountain? What fit return can we make for your kindness in dedicating to Us so noble a product of your intellect?

Both considerations exceed the powers of language, or even of thought; nor can we reflect on your services and deserts without being overcome.

What love, what zeal is yours for the defence of Christian Faith! What benevolence in Our regard! And in the book itself, what solidity of matter, clearness of method, force of eloquence, wherein the Holy Spirit Himself shows visibly!

It is thoroughly judicious, wise, and pious; charitable in instruction, gentle in admonition, correct in argument. If there be any of your opponents who have not fallen entirely into the power of the Prince of Darkness, they must be drawn by your writings to a saner condition of mind, if any chance for sanity be left.

These are distinguished and admirable achievements; and as they have been wrought in a new fashion, by a princely favour, for Almighty God and the Holy See, we render you, Defender of the Faith, unbounded thanks.

The Apostolic See thanks you; all who worship Christ and unite in His faith thank you. We, for Our part, with the concurrence of Our venerable brothers, bestow on you, in other letters sealed with lead, as you will find from their perusal, this title of Defender of the Faith.

For your part, most dear Son, however you may consider great and desirable these honours which the Holy Apostolic See grants you as a reward of eminent virtue and a mark of its grateful appreciation, realise that greater and more glorious compensation is prepared for you in heaven by Our Lord and Saviour.

In upholding His cause and His spouse by every means of defence you have displayed your spirit and your virtue; and while you review those titles which you have acquired on earth and in heaven, remember by what claims you have gained them.

Show yourself hereafter such as you have been heretofore. Let your later deeds be equal to your sublime and glorious beginnings. Let the Apostolic See, once defended by your arms, and the Christian Faith, now fortified by the shield of your doctrine against the criminal frenzy of heretics, find and prove you ever a helper in all their perils, so that this extraordinary and unspeakable glory which Your Majesty has most mightily merited by your great efforts may continue to the last day of your life and endure to all future time as a theme of eulogy.

Given at Rome, at St. Peter's, under the seal of the Fisherman, the fourth day of November, 1521, the ninth year of Our Pontificate.

The Epistle Dedicatory

To our Most Holy Lord Leo X, Head Bishop, Henry King of England, France, and Ireland, wishes perpetual happiness.

Most Holy Father:

Perhaps it may appear strange to Your Holiness, that part of our youth being spent in martial affairs, and part in the studies of things belonging to the Commonwealth; we should now undertake the task of a man, that ought to have employed all his time in the studies of learning; in opposing Ourself against this growing heresy.

But Your Holiness (I suppose) will the less admire, when You consider the reasons that obliged Us to take upon Us this charge of writing.

We have seen tares cast into our Lord's Harvest (Matt. 13:25); sects do spring up, and heresies increase so much as almost, to overthrow the Faith of Christ.

Such seeds of discord are sown abroad in the world, that no sincere Christian, can suffer, or endure any longer their spreading mischief, without an obligation of employing all his studies and forces to oppose them.

Your Holiness ought not, therefore, to wonder, if We (not the greatest in ability, yet in Faith and good-will inferior to none) have proposed to Ourself, to employ our force and power in a work so necessary, and so profitable, that it cannot lightly be omitted by any, without offence; also to declare Our great respect towards Your Holiness, Our endeavours for the propagation of the Faith of Christ, and Our obedience to the service of Almighty God: greatly confiding, that although our learning is not much, nay in comparison, even nothing; yet His Grace will so co-operate with Us, that what we are not able thereby to effect, He, by his Benignity and Power, may more fully perform, and by his Strength supply Our weakness therein.

Though we know very well, that there are everywhere several more expert, especially in Holy Writ, who could have more commodiously undertaken this great work, and performed it much better than We: Yet are We not altogether so ignorant, as not to esteem it Our duty, to employ, with all Our might, Our wit and pen in the common Cause.

For having, by long experience, found, that Religion bears the greatest sway in the administration of public affairs, and is likewise of no small importance in the Commonwealth; We have employed no little time, especially since We came to years of discretion, in the contemplation thereof; wherein We have always taken great delight.

And though not ignorant of Our small progress therein made; yet, at least, it is so much, as, We hope, (especially with the help, or rather instigation of such things as can instruct the most ignorant, viz. piety, and the grief of seeing Religion abused) will suffice for reasons to discover the subtleties of Luther's heresy.

We have therefore, (confiding in those things) entered upon this work; dedicating to Your Holiness what We have meditated therein; that, under Your protection, who are Christ's Vicar upon Earth, it may pass the public censure.

For we are persuaded that this heresy, having for some time exercised its rage amongst Christians; and being by Your most weighty and wholesome sentence condemned, and, as it were, by force plucked out of men's hands, if anything remains hidden in the bowels of it, fed by flattery and fair promises; it is to be rooted out by just reasons, and arguments; that, as men's wits suffer themselves more willingly to be led than drawn; so reason also may supply these with the mildest remedies.

Whether or no anything is effectually done in this, shall rest to Your Holiness' Judgment: If We have erred in anything, We offer it to be corrected as may please Your Holiness.

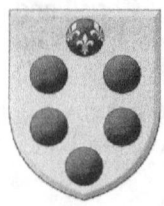

The Papal Bull

Leo X, Bishop and Servant of the Servants of God:

To our most dear son in Christ, Henry the illustrious King of England, and Defender of the Faith, sends greeting, and gives his benediction.

By the good pleasure and will of Almighty God, presiding in the government of the Universal Church, though unworthy so great charge, We daily employ all our thoughts, both at home and abroad, for the continual propagation of the Holy Catholic Faith, without which none can be saved.

And that the methods which are taken for repressing of such as labour to overthrow the Church, or pervert, and stain Her by wicked glosses, and malicious lies; may be carried on with continual profit, as is ordered by the sound doctrine of the faithful, and especially of such as shine in the regal dignity: We employ with all our power, our endeavours, and all the parts of our ministry.

And as the other Roman Bishops, our Predecessors, have been accustomed to bestow some particular favours upon Catholic Princes, as the exigencies of affairs and times required, especially on those who, in tempestuous times, and whilst the rapid perfidiousness of schismatics and heretics raged, not only persevered constantly in the true Faith, and unspotted devotion of the Holy Roman Catholic Church; but also as the legitimate sons and stoutest champions of the same, have opposed themselves, both spiritually and temporally, against the mad fury of schismatics and heretics.

So also, We, for your Majesty's most excellent works, and worthy actions done for Us, and this Holy See, in which by divine permission we preside; do desire to confer upon your Majesty, with honour and immortal praises, that, which may enable and engage you carefully to drive away from our Lord's Flock the wolves; and cut off with the material sword, the rotten members that infect the mystical Body of Jesus Christ, and confirm the hearts of the almost discomforted faithful in the solidity of Faith.

Truly, when our beloved son John Clark, your Majesty's Orator, did lately in our Consistory, in presence of our venerable brethren, Cardinals of the sacred Roman Church, and divers others holy Prelates, present unto Us a book, which Your Majesty, moved by your charity (which effects everything readily and well) and enflamed with zeal to the holy Catholic Faith, and fervour of devotion towards Us, and this Holy See; did compose, as a most noble and wholesome antidote against the errors of divers heretics, often condemned by this Holy See, and now again revived by Martin Luther.

When, I say, he offered this Book to Us, to be examined, and approved by Our authority, and also declared in a very eloquent discourse, that as Your Majesty had by true reasons and the undeniable authority of Scripture and the holy Fathers, confuted the notorious errors of Luther; so you are likewise ready, and resolved to prosecute, with all the forces of your Kingdom, those who shall presume to follow, or defend them; having found in this book most admirable doctrine, sprinkled with the dew of divine grace.

We rendered infinite thanks to Almighty God, from whom every good thing, and every perfect gift proceeds, for being pleased to fill with His grace, and to inspire your most excellent mind, inclined to all good, to defend, by your writings, His Holy Faith, against the new broacher of those condemned errors; and to invite all other Christians, by your example, to assist and favour, with all their power, the orthodox Faith, and evangelical Truth, now under so great peril and danger.

Considering that it is but just, that those who undertake pious labours in defence of the Faith of Christ should be extolled with all praise and honour; and being willing, not only to magnify with deserved praise, and approve with our authority, what your Majesty has with learning and eloquence written against Luther; but also to honour your Majesty with such a title, as shall give all Christians to understand, as well in our times, as in succeeding ages, how acceptable and welcome your gift was to Us, especially in this juncture of time.

We, the true Successor of Saint Peter - whom Christ, before His Ascension, left as his Vicar upon Earth, and to whom He committed the care of His Flock - presiding in this Holy See, from whence all dignity and titles have their source, have with our brethren maturely deliberated on these things and with one consent unanimously decreed to bestow on your Majesty this title, viz. Defender of the Faith.

And, as we have by this title honoured you; we likewise command all Christians, that they name your Majesty by this title; and that in their writings to your Majesty, immediately after the word KING, they add, DEFENDER OF THE FAITH.

Having thus weighed, and diligently considered your singular merits, we could not have invented a more congruous name, nor more worthy of Your Majesty, than this worthy and most excellent title; which, as often as you hear, or read, you shall remember your own merits and virtues: nor will you, by this title, exalt yourself, or become proud, but, according to your accustomed prudence, rather more humble in the Faith of Christ, and more strong and constant in your devotion to this Holy See, by which you were exalted.

And you shall rejoice in our Lord, who is the Giver of all good things, for leaving such a perpetual and everlasting monument of your glory to posterity, and showing the way to others, that if they also covet to be invested with such a title, they may study to do such actions, and to follow the steps of your most excellent Majesty; whom, with your wife, children, and all who shall spring from you, We bless with a bountiful and liberal hand, in the Name of Him from whom the power of benediction is given to Us, and by whom Kings reign, and Princes govern; and in whose hands are the hearts of Kings.

Praying, and beseeching the most High, to confirm your Majesty in your most holy purposes, and to augment your devotion, and for your most excellent deeds in defence of His Holy Faith, to render your Majesty so illustrious and famous to the whole world, as that our judgment in adorning you with so remarkable a title, may not be thought vain, or light, by any person whatsoever.

And finally, after you have finished your course in this life, that He may make you partaker of His eternal glory.

It shall not be lawful for any person whatsoever, to infringe, or by any rash presumption to act contrary to this letter of subscribing, and command. But, if any one shall presume to make such attempt, let him know, that he shall thereby incur the indignation of Almighty God, and of the holy Apostles, Peter and Paul.

Given at St. Peter's in Rome, the fifth of the Ides of October, in the Year of Our Lord's Incarnation 1521, and in the ninth Year of our Papacy.

Leo X. PP

HENRY VIII.

ourteous Reader, in this little book I hope I have clearly demonstrated how absurdly and impiously Luther has handled the Holy Sacraments.

I hope I have made clear how rashly Luther calumniates the Church, and how impertinent, how impious, and how absurd he is against the holy Fathers; against Scriptures; against the public faith of the Church; against the consent of so many ages and people; even against common sense itself.

I wish he may at last repent himself for having treated of Penance in so evil a manner, that he may wholesomely perform all its parts, since he endeavours to destroy them all; that he may be contrite for his malice and publicly confess his errors; and that by submitting himself to the judgement of the Church – which he has offended with so many blasphemies - he may atone for what he has committed with the greatest satisfaction possible.

I indeed abhor this man's great madness and most lamentable state and I wish that even now - God inspiring him by grace – he may at length come to his senses, be converted and live.

I beseech and entreat all other Christians, by the Heart of Christ, Whose Faith we profess, to turn their ears away from those impious words and not foster schisms and discords, especially at this time when it behoves Christians most particularly to be united against the enemies of Christ.

Henry VIII

ASSERTIO SE,
ptē Sacramētorū ad,
uersus Marti. Lu,
therū, ædita ab in,
uictissimo An,
gliæ & Frāciæ
rege, & do.
Hyberniæ Henrico
eius nominis
octauo.

To the Reader

 I DO NOT RANK myself among the most learned and eloquent. Yet, in order to avoid the fault of ingratitude and moved by fidelity and piety, I am obliged to defend my Mother, the Spouse of Christ.[1]

Would to God my ability to do it were equal to my good will!

---

[1] [The Church] is called the "Bride of Christ" because the Lord himself called himself her "Spouse" (Mark 2:19). The Lord has loved the Church and has joined her to himself in an everlasting covenant. He has given himself up for her in order to purify her with his blood and "sanctify her" (Ephesians 5:26), making her the fruitful mother of all the children of God. While the term "body" expresses the unity of the "head" with the members, the term "bride" emphasises the distinction of the two in their personal relationship (*Compendium*, Number 158).

Although the duty to defend the Church is incumbent upon the most learned – and this is a subject more copiously handled by others - I account it as much my own duty to oppose, with my utmost endeavours, the poisonous shafts of the enemy that fights against Her.

When no one assaulted the Church in the past, it was not necessary to resist. But the present state of things requires this of me at this point in time. [2]

Now the enemy, the most wicked enemy imaginable, is risen up: he spews out the poison of vipers against the Church and the Catholic Faith by the instigation of the devil, under pretext of charity and stimulated by anger and hatred.

It is necessary that every servant of Christ, of whatever age, gender, or order, should rise against this common enemy of the Christian Faith, so that those whose power does not avail anyone, may yet testify their good will by their good efforts. [3]

Therefore, it is now fitting that we arm ourselves with a twofold armour: one heavenly, and the other earthly.

A heavenly armour, so that he who by a feigned and dissembled charity destroys others and perishes himself may be gained by true charity.

Thus, being so gained, he may also gain others and be conquered by true Doctrine, since he fights by a false doctrine.

An earthly armour, so that if he is so obstinately malicious as to neglect holy Councils and despise God's reproofs, he may be constrained by due punishments.

Thus, so that he who will not do good may stop doing mischief, (Rom. 13: 3-4) and he that did harm by the word of malice may do good by the example of his punishments.

What plague so pernicious did ever invade the Flock of Christ?

---

[2] The Christian faithful are those who, inasmuch as they have been incorporated in Christ through Baptism, have been constituted as the people of God; for this reason, since they have become sharers in Christ's priestly, prophetic and royal office in their own manner, they are called to exercise the mission which God has entrusted to the Church. There exists a true equality among them in their dignity as children of God (*Compendium*, Number 177).

[3] The laity participates in the prophetic office by welcoming evermore in faith the Word of Christ and proclaiming it to the world by the witness of their lives, their words, their evangelizing action, and by catechesis. This evangelizing action acquires a particular efficacy because it is accomplished in the ordinary circumstances of the world (*Compendium*, Number 190).

What serpent so venomous has crept in, as the one who wrote the *'Babylonian Captivity of the Church'*?

It is he who:

Wrests Holy Scripture by his own sense, against the Sacraments of Christ;

Abolishes the ecclesiastical Rites and Ceremonies left by the Fathers;

Undervalues the holy and ancient Interpreters of Scripture, unless they concur with his sentiments;

Calls the most Holy See of Rome, 'Babylon', and the Pope's authority, 'tyranny';

Regards the most wholesome Decrees of the Universal Church to be 'Captivity';

Turns the name of the most Holy Bishop of Rome, to that of 'Antichrist'?

O, that detestable trumpeter of pride, calumnies and schisms!

What kind of infernal wolf is he, who seeks to disperse the Flock of Christ (Matt.7:15)?

What great a member of the Devil is he (John 8:44), who endeavours to tear the Christian members of Christ from their Head?

How infectious is his soul, who revives these detestable opinions and buried schisms, and adds new ones to the old?

He who, like Cerberus from hell, brings to light the heresies which ought to lie in eternal darkness?

He, who considers himself worthy to govern all things by his own word, opposes the judgments of all the Ancients?

Nay, also to ruin the Church of God! [4]

I do not know what to say of his malice, for I think neither tongue nor pen can express its enormity.

Wherefore, by the Name of Christ which we profess, I exhort, pray and beseech all Christians who are willing to look upon and read Luther's works, especially the *'Babylonian Captivity'* - if he is its author - to do it cautiously, and very wisely.

Virgil said that he gathered gold out of the dross of Ennius; so Christians may likewise gather good things out of evil.

---

[4] The word Church refers to the people whom God calls and gathers together from every part of the earth. They form the assembly of those who through faith and Baptism have become children of God, members of Christ, and temples of the Holy Spirit (*Compendium*, Number. 147).

If anything pleases them, let them not be so absorbed by it so as to suck the poison with the honey, for it is better to be without both than to swallow both.

To prevent this danger, I wish the author may repent, be converted, and live (Ezech. 33:11).

In imitation of St. Augustine, whose Rule Luther professed, may he correct his books so filled with malice and revoke his errors.

If he refuses this and if Christian Princes do their duty, it will shortly come to pass that these errors may be burned in the fire and he himself, if he perseveres in them.

In the meanwhile, we thought it fit to expose to the readers some chief heads or chapters in the *'Babylonian Captivity'* which contain the most venom, whereby it will appear very clearly with what exulcerated mind he began this work, pretending the public good, but writing nothing but malicious inventions.

We need not seek any extraordinary testimonies to prove what we have said, for Luther, fearing that anyone should go up and down in search of such, uncovers himself and his mind of his own accord in his very beginning.

For who, upon reading this one sentence of his, should doubt what he aimed at:

Indulgentiae sunt adulatorum Romanorum nequitiae.
(Indulgences are iniquities of the Roman flatterers)

Chapter I

Of Indulgences

Indulgentiae sunt adulatorum Romanorum nequitiae.
(Indulgences are iniquities of the Roman flatterers)

VERY LIVING creature is known chiefly by its face, so by this first proposition it evidently appears how corrupt and rotten Luther's heart was; he whose mouth, being filled with bitterness, broke out into such a corruption.

To many, what he said of Indulgences [5] in times past seemed to detract much from the Roman Bishop's power.

It also lessened the good hope and holy consolation of the faithful, excited men greatly to trust in the riches of their own penitence and to despise the treasures of the Holy Church and the Bounty of God.

And yet what he wrote then was favourably interpreted, because he only disputed many of them, but did not affirm them, desiring to be taught and promising to obey him who would instruct him better.

But what this new *saint* then wrote with a simple intention is easily laid bare - he who refers all things to the Holy Spirit, Who cannot brook anything of falsehood.

As soon as he had any wholesome advice given him, he immediately vomited his malediction against those who endeavoured to do him good, reviling them with reproaches and quarrels.

It is worth our while to see what height of folly he has come to at last.

He previously confessed that Indulgences were good, to at least absolve us from both the crime and the punishments which should be enjoined us by the order of the Church, or by our particular priest.

But now it was not by learning but by mere malice that he laboured against the Holy Church. [6]

Thus, contradicting himself, he condemns Indulgences and says, *'they are nothing but mere impostures, fit only to destroy people's money, and God's Faith.'*

Everyone can see how wickedly and furiously he rails in this matter: If Indulgences, as he says, are but mere impostures and good for nothing, then it follows that our Pope Leo X is an impostor!

---

[5] Indulgences are the remission before God of the temporal punishment due to sins whose guilt has already been forgiven. The faithful Christian who is duly disposed gains the indulgence under prescribed conditions for either himself or the departed. Indulgences are granted through the ministry of the Church which, as the dispenser of the grace of redemption, distributes the treasury of the merits of Christ and the Saints (*Compendium*, No. 312).

[6] The Church is the community in which the Christian receives the Word of God, the teachings of the "Law of Christ" (Galatians 6:2), and the grace of the sacraments. Christians are united to the Eucharistic sacrifice of Christ in such a way that their moral life is an act of spiritual worship; and they learn the example of holiness from the Virgin Mary and the lives of the Saints (*Compendium*, Number 429).

Leo X, whose innocent, unspotted life and most holy conversation are well known throughout the world, as Luther himself confesses in a letter of his to the Pope.

Nay, all Roman Bishops in so many past ages are likewise impostors. They who used to grant Indulgences, as Luther himself says: some a year's remission; some three years; some to forgive a Lenten penance; some a certain part of the whole penance; as the third, or one-half; at least something as to plenary, or full remission of the sin and punishment.

They were all impostors, if Luther speaks the truth.

But how much more reason is there to believe that this *little brother* is himself a scabbed sheep, rather than so many pastors were treacherous and unfaithful?

For Luther, as is said above, shows what kind of man he is, and how uncharitable, when he is not embarrassed to lay such a crime against so great and holy Bishops. [7]

If God says to all, *'thou shalt not be a detractor nor a whisperer among the people'* (Lev. 19:16), what may we think of Luther, who casts such a foul scandal, not only on one man, but also on so many venerable prelates?

And this he murmurs, not only in one city, but publishes to the whole world.

If he is accursed *'who secretly killeth his neighbour'* (Deut. 27:24), with how great a curse shall he be stricken who insults his Authorities with such reproaches?

Finally, if, as the Gospel says, *'whosoever hateth his brother is a murderer. And you know that no murderer hath eternal life abiding in himself'* (1 John 3:15), does not this parricide deserve everlasting death for persecuting his Father with such hatred?

---

[7] The Church is holy insofar as the Most Holy God is her author. Christ has given himself for her to sanctify her and make her a source of sanctification. The Holy Spirit gives her life with charity. In the Church one finds the fullness of the means of salvation. Holiness is the vocation of each of her members and the purpose of all her activities. The Church counts among her members the Virgin Mary and numerous Saints who are her models and intercessors. The holiness of the Church is the fountain of sanctification for her children who here on earth recognize themselves as sinners ever in need of conversion and purification (*Compendium*, Number 165).

Seeing that Luther has come to deny Indulgences to be profitable in this life, it would be in vain for me to dispute what great benefits the souls in Purgatory [8] receive from them.

Moreover, what would it avail us to discourse with him of the great helps whereby we are relieved from Purgatory itself?

Unable to endure hearing that the Pope delivers any person out of Purgatory, [9] Luther presumes to leave no one there himself.

What profit is there to dispute, or fight against Luther, who fights against himself?

What should my arguments avail me, even though I forced him to confess what he previously denied, since he now denies what he previously confessed?

Even if it is admitted that the Pope's Indulgences were questionable, it is necessary that the words of Christ remain firm, whereby He gave the keys of the Church to Saint Peter, when He said: *'whatsoever thou shalt bind upon earth, it shall be bound also in heaven: and whatsoever thou shalt loose on earth, it shall be loosed also in heaven'* (Matt 16:19).

Likewise, *'whose sins you shall forgive, they are forgiven them: and whose sins you shall retain, they are retained'* (John 20:23).

Thus, if it is manifest that any priest has power to absolve men from sins and take away eternal punishment due to them, who will not judge it ridiculous that the Prince of all priests should be denied the taking away of temporal punishment?

But some may say that perhaps Luther will not admit that any priest has the power of binding or loosing anything, or that the Pope has any greater power than other Bishops or priests.

But of what concern is it to me what Luther admits, or denies?

He who granted many things a while ago, which now he denies? And he who, alone, rejects all things which the Holy Church has held during so many ages?

---

[8] Purgatory is the state of those who die in God's friendship, assured of their eternal salvation, but who still have need of purification to enter into the happiness of heaven (*Compendium*, Number 210).

[9] Because of the communion of saints, the faithful who are still pilgrims on earth are able to help the souls in purgatory by offering prayers in suffrage for them, especially the Eucharistic sacrifice. They also help them by almsgiving, indulgences, and works of penance. (*Compendium*, No. 211).

Leaving aside other things that this new Momus, or feigned deity, censures, it is certain that, if the Popes have erred in granting Indulgences, then the whole congregation of the faithful are not free from sin, since they received Indulgences for so long a time, and with so great ease. [10]

I do not doubt that we may agree with the Pope's judgment and the custom observed by the Saints, rather than with Luther alone.

He, who furiously condemns the whole Church and loads its Bishops with mad reproaches, does not fear to publish that the supremacy of the Pope is but a vain name, and effectually nothing but the Kingdom of Babylon and the power of Nimrod, that strong hunter.

Luther now desires his readers and bookbinders to burn whatsoever he first wrote on the Papacy and reserve this one proposition, namely,

Papatus est robusta Venatio Romani Pontificis
(The Papacy is the strong Game of the Roman Pontiff)

---

[10] The communion of saints also refers to the communion between holy persons (sancti); that is, between those who by grace are united to the dead and risen Christ. Some are pilgrims on the earth; others, having passed from this life, are undergoing purification and are helped also by our prayers. Others already enjoy the glory of God and intercede for us. All of these together form in Christ one family, the Church, to the praise and glory of the Trinity (*Compendium*, Number 195).

Chapter II

Of the Pope's Authority

Papatus est robusta Venatio Romani Pontificis
(The Papacy is the strong Game of the Roman Pontiff)

INDEED IT IS no ridiculous desire of Luther that the things he wrote previously should be burned, because many of them deserved it.

Yet much more should this new proposition of his be destroyed by fire, which he desires to be preserved after the rest are burned, as though it were worthy of eternity.

What man, if he had not known his malice, would not be startled at his inconstancy in this matter?

In the first place, he denied the Pope's Supremacy to be of divine right or Law and allowed it to be of human right. [11]

But now, contradicting himself, he affirms it to be of neither of them, but rather that the Papacy has assumed and usurped tyranny by mere force.

Formerly he was of the opinion that power over the Universal Church was given to Roman Bishops by human consent, and for the public good.

He was so much of that opinion that he detested the schism of the Bohemians - who denied any obedience to the See of Rome - saying that *'they sinned damnably who did not obey the Pope.'*

Shortly after having written these things, Luther embraces now what he detested then.

The same *stability* he has in this: after he preached in a sermon to the people that *'excommunication is a medicine, and to be suffered with patience and obedience';* he himself, a while after being justly excommunicated, was so impatient of that sentence that, mad with rage, he broke forth into intolerable quarrels, reproaches and blasphemies.

So, by his fury, it plainly appears that those who are driven from the bosom of their Holy Mother Church are immediately seized, possessed with furies and tormented by devils.

But I ask this: since he saw these things such a short while ago, how is it that he is now of the opinion that he saw nothing at all?

What new eyes has he got? Is his sight sharper, after he has joined anger to his wonted pride and added hatred to both? Does he see further with such *excellent* spectacles?

I will not offend the Bishop of Rome so much as to troublesomely or closely dispute his right, as if it were a doubtful matter.

It is sufficient for my present task to show that the enemy is led by so much fury, that he destroys his own credit.

---

[11] The Pope, Bishop of Rome and the Successor of Saint Peter, is the perpetual, visible source and foundation of the unity of the Church. He is the Vicar of Christ, the head of the College of bishops and pastor of the universal Church over which he has by divine institution full, supreme, immediate, and universal power (*Compendium*, Number 182).

He clearly demonstrates that, being so blinded by mere malice, he neither sees nor knows what he says himself.

He cannot deny that all the faithful honour and acknowledge the sacred Roman See as their Mother and Supreme; nor does distance of place or dangers in the way hinder access to Her. [12]

For example: if those who come hither from the Indies tell us the truth, the Indians - who themselves are separated from us by such a vast distance, both of land and sea - do submit to the See of Rome. [13]

If the Bishop of Rome wields this great power, neither by command of God nor the will of man, but by sheer force, I would fain ask of Luther: when did the Pope rush into the possession of such great privileges?

So vast a power cannot have had an obscure origin, especially if its beginning is remembered by man.

But perhaps Luther will say that it is above one or two ages since: then let him point out the exact time by historical records.

Otherwise, if the beginning of so great a thing is so ancient that it is quite forgotten; let him know that, by all man's standards, we must believe that it had a lawful beginning and are not allowed to think otherwise. This beginning so far surpasses the memory of man that its origin is not known.

It is certain that by the unanimous consent of all nations, it is forbidden to change or move the things which have been immoveable for a long time.

Truly, if any one will look upon ancient monuments, or read the History of former times, one may easily find that all Churches in Christendom have been obedient to the See of Rome since the conversion of the world.

---

[12] The Church is catholic, that is, universal, insofar as Christ is present in her: *"Where there is Christ Jesus, there is the Catholic Church"* (Saint Ignatius of Antioch). The Church proclaims the fullness and the totality of the faith; she bears and administers the fullness of the means of salvation; she is sent out by Christ on a mission to the whole of the human race (*Compendium*, No. 166).

[13] The Church, although made up of persons who have diverse languages, cultures, and rites, nonetheless professes with a united voice the one faith that was received from the one Lord and that was passed on by the one Apostolic Tradition. She confesses one God alone, Father, Son, and Holy Spirit, and points to one way of salvation. Therefore we believe with one heart and one soul all that is contained in the Word of God, handed down or written, and which is proposed by the Church as divinely revealed (*Compendium*, Number 32).

We find that, though the Empire was transferred to the Greeks, they still held and obeyed the Supremacy of the Church and the See of Rome, except when they were in turbulent schism.

St. Jerome, though not a Roman himself, demonstrates admirably well his good esteem for the Roman See, when he openly declared that *'it was sufficient for him that the Pope of Rome approved his Faith, whoever else should disapprove it'*.

Luther, going against his former sentence, impudently asserts that *'the Pope has no right of any kind over the Catholic Church; no, not so much as human; but has by mere force tyrannically usurped it'*.

I am astonished that he should expect his readers to be so easily induced to believe his words.

Who would be so blockish as to think that a priest could ever expect or hope to obtain so great a power over so many of his fellow Bishops in so many different and diverse nations before he enjoyed that right which Luther says he usurped?

And this without any right or title, weapon or company to defend him, as the Pope doubtlessly was.

How, I say, could Luther expect anybody to believe that all nations and cities - nay, all kingdoms and provinces - were so prodigal of their rights and liberties, as to acknowledge the superiority of a strange priest, to whom they should owe no subjection?

I do not know how he could desire they should.

But what does it mean to know Luther's opinion in this case, when, through anger and malice he is ignorant of his own opinion, or of what he thinks himself?

In doing and saying such inconsistent things he manifestly uncovers the darkness of his understanding and knowledge, and the folly and blindness of his heart, abandoned as it is to a reprobate sense.

How true is that saying of the Apostle? *'If I should have prophecy and should know all mysteries, and all knowledge, and if I should have all faith, so that I could remove mountains, and have not charity, I am nothing'* (1 Cor.13:2).

By perishing himself through fury, Luther not only shows how void of this charity he is, and even more by endeavouring to draw all others with him into destruction, he strives to dissuade them from their obedience to the Pope, whom, in a three-fold manner, he himself is bound to obey, viz., as a Christian, as a priest, and as a religious brother.

His disobedience also deserves to be punished in a treble manner:

He does not remember how much *'obedience is better than sacrifice'* (1 Kings 15:22);

He does not consider how it is ordained in Deuteronomy, that *'he that will be proud, and refuse to obey the commandment of the priest, who ministers at that time to the Lord thy God, and the decree of the judge, that man shall die, and thou shalt take away the evil from Israel'* (Deut. 17:12);

He does not consider, I say, what cruel punishment he deserves, who will not obey the High Priest and Supreme Judge upon earth.

This *poor brother*, being cited to appear before the Pope - who offered to pay his expenses and a promise of safe conduct - refused to go without a guard, troubling the whole Church as much as he could and exciting the whole Body to rebel against the Head.

To do this is like the sin of witchcraft, and to concur, is as the sin of idolatry (1 Kings 15:22).

Moved by hatred, Luther runs head-long on to destruction and refuses to submit to the Law of God, desiring to establish a law of his own.

Thus, it behoves all Christians to beware lest, as the Apostle says, *'by the disobedience of one man, many were made sinners'* (Rom. 5:19).

On the contrary, by hating and detesting his wickedness, we may sing with the Prophet, *'I have hated the unjust, and have loved Thy Law'* (Ps. 118:113).

Chapter III

The Defence of the Seven Sacraments

I HAVE ALREADY given my view on these two chapters, namely, on abrogating indulgences and taking all authority away from the Pope.

Although they are wicked, these two chapters are but the first flourishing or essays of Luther, who now begins to murder and destroy the Sacraments in his book.

He confesses this whole book of his to be but a flourish - I do not know to what work: I suppose it is some work in which he intends to fight more seriously against our most holy Faith.

Yet, I am much amazed that he should think to compose anything whatsoever more venomous than this whole preface or flourish of his.

Because, of the seven Sacraments he leaves us only three. [14]

He also tells us that those three will not stay long either, except for a time, and he shall soon also take them from us.

From the three, he immediately takes one away in the same book, whereby he plainly shows us what he intends to do with the rest.

It seems that he prepares the way to this task when he says that if he would speak according to Scripture, he would leave but one Sacrament and three Sacramental signs.

If anyone diligently examines how Luther handles these three Sacraments - which, for the present, he puts as three Sacraments, or under three signs - one may realise that he treats them in such a manner that no one should doubt that, when he sees his own time, at his own pleasure, he intends wholly to deprive us of them all.

Let you, the reader, diligently observe Luther's steps, and watch your own, that you may discover the subtleties of this serpent.

And let you not, being too overconfident, thrust yourself amongst these thorns, brambles, and dens, but rather cautiously walk round his caverns, fearing lest he should secretly strike his mortal sting into your heel.

Once this hideous monster is caught, he will become benumbed, and pine away by his own venom.

---

[14] The sacraments, instituted by Christ and entrusted to the Church, are efficacious signs of grace perceptible to the senses. Through them divine life is bestowed upon us. There are seven sacraments: Baptism, Confirmation, Holy Eucharist, Penance, Anointing of the Sick, Holy Orders, and Matrimony (*Compendium*, Number 224).

Chapter IV

The Sacrament of the Altar

ET US THEREFORE begin where he began himself, with the adorable Sacrament of Christ's Body.

By changing its name and calling it *The Sacrament of Bread*, Luther shows that he cannot well bear that we should refer to Christ's Body by the name of the *Blessed Sacrament*. [15]

---

[15] The unfathomable richness of this sacrament is expressed in different names which evoke its various aspects. The most common names are: the Eucharist, Holy Mass, the Lord's Supper, the Breaking of the Bread, the Eucharistic Celebration, the Memorial of the passion, death and Resurrection of the Lord, the Holy Sacrifice, the Holy and Divine Liturgy, the Sacred Mysteries,

He also shows that, if it were possible for him under any reasonable pretext, he would give it a worse name.

How much does the judgment of St. Ambrose differ from this man's, when he says, *'though the form of the bread and wine is seen upon the Altar, yet we must believe that there is nothing else but the Body and Blood of Christ'*.

By these words, it clearly appears that St. Ambrose confesses that no other substance remains with the Body and Blood of Christ in the Sacrament, when he says, *'that which is seen under the form of bread and wine is nothing else but the Body and Blood of Christ'*. [16]

If St. Ambrose had only said *Flesh* and *Blood* without adding anything else, perhaps Luther would have said that the bread and wine were there also, as he himself says that *'the substance of the Flesh is with the bread, and the substance of the Blood along with the wine'*.

But seeing that St. Ambrose says that *'there is nothing else but the Body and Blood'*, it appears that he is manifestly against Luther, who affirms that *'the Bread is with the Flesh, and the Wine with the Blood'*.

Even if what Luther falsely says were true, that *'the Bread should remain mingled with the Body of Christ'*, it was not necessary for him to blot out of the Sacrament the name of the Body of Christ, in which he confesses that the true Body of Christ is.

If the substance of bread should be with the Body of Christ - as he contends - there is no reason that the inferior substance - bread - should take away the name from the more worthy one - Body.

When the Apostle called it 'bread', he was conforming himself to the understanding of the hearers, who were then ignorant people.

Nevertheless, nowadays, after the Faith has been so long established, it was not fit or convenient to change this so adorable a name - Body of Christ - into a name that would have turned their minds from the Body to the bread.

---

the Most Holy Sacrament of the Altar, and Holy Communion (*Compendium*, Number 275).

[16] Jesus Christ is present in the Eucharist in a unique and incomparable way. He is present in a true, real and substantial way, with his Body and his Blood, with his Soul and his Divinity. In the Eucharist, therefore, there is present in a sacramental way, that is, under the Eucharistic species of bread and wine, Christ whole and entire, God and Man (*Compendium*, No. 282).

For this name represents to the hearers the thing in the Sacrament. [17]

Undoubtedly, Luther would not have changed it, if he had not determined with himself to draw the people to worship the bread and leave out Christ's Body, from which he himself is divided.

I shall presently speak more fully concerning this.

---

[17] The Eucharist is the very sacrifice of the Body and Blood of the Lord Jesus which he instituted to perpetuate the sacrifice of the cross throughout the ages until his return in glory. Thus he entrusted to his Church this memorial of his death and Resurrection. It is a sign of unity, a bond of charity, a paschal banquet, in which Christ is consumed, the mind is filled with grace, and a pledge of future glory is given to us (Compendium, Number 271).

The Sacrament of the Eucharist under one form only administered to the laity

 N THE MEANWHILE, let us truly examine how subtly, under pretence of favouring the laity, Luther endeavours to stir them up to hatred against the clergy.
He resolved to cast a suspicion over the Church's faith so that Her authority should be of no consequence against him.

To this end, he began with that one question that he foresaw would be praised and applauded by the people: he touched the old sore, whereby

Bohemia had been formerly blistered - that is, *'the laity ought to receive the Eucharist under both kinds.'*

Thus, he opened that wound in order that he might destroy the principal mysteries of Christianity.

When first he began to handle this point, he only said *'that the Pope would do well to have it ordained by a general Council that the laity should receive the Sacrament under both kinds.'*

However, when some disputed that with him and denied his opinion, he did not content himself to stop there, but rather grew to such a perverse height that he condemned the whole clergy of wickedness for withholding the other Species without consent of any Council.

For my part, I do not dispute the first opinion. For to me there appears to be no reason why the Church should not ordain the Sacrament to be administered to the laity under both kinds.

However, I do not doubt that it was very appropriate what was done in times past, in omitting it and also in hindering it to be so administered now.

I cannot believe the whole clergy, during so many ages, to have been so void of sense as to incur eternal punishment for a thing by which they could reap no temporal good.

Furthermore, it does not appear that such a danger exists. God not only bestowed heaven upon those men, who did it themselves and wrote that it ought to be done, but likewise, He had them honoured on earth by those whom He is adored Himself.

Amongst them - to mention but two - was that most learned and holy man Thomas Aquinas, whom I very willingly name here.

The wickedness of Luther cannot endure the sanctity of this man whom all Christians honour; Luther reviles Aquinas with his foul lips.

There are very many, though not canonised, who are contrary to Luther's opinion in this and to whom Luther is not comparable in any way in piety and learning.

Among them is the Master of the Sentences, Nicholas de Lyra (and many others), to each of whom it behoves all Christians to give more credit than to Luther.

But pray observe how Luther staggers, and contradicts himself:

In one place, he says that *'Christ, in His Last Supper, not only said to all the faithful, as permitting, but as commanding, 'Drink ye all of this'* (Matt. 26:27).

Afterwards, fearing to offend the laity - whom he flatters with a view to stir up their hatred against the priests - he adds these words: *'they who* use but one kind do not sin against Christ, seeing that Christ did not command to use any kind, but left it to every man's discretion, saying, 'As often as ye do this, do it in remembrance of Me.'

'*But*, says Luther, *they sin who forbid giving both kinds to such as are willing to receive them.*'

'*The blame, says he, lies on the clergy, and not on the laity.*'

You see how clearly he first holds it for a command, and then says: it is no commandment, but something left to every man's discretion.

What need is there for us to contradict Luther, he who so often contradicts himself?

And yet before, when he spoke of all in general, he did not defend the laity well, if anyone would urge the matter. He proves that there is no sin in the priests, whom he accuses most bitterly.

Because, says he, '*the sin consists in the priest's taking the liberty of one kind from the laity*'.

If anybody should ask him, how does he know that the custom has been practised against the people's will? I believe he cannot tell.

Why, then, does he condemn the whole clergy, for having taken the laity's right from them by force, seeing he cannot by any testimony prove that this was forcibly done?

How much more reasonable should it be to say that the consent of the people did concur with this custom for so many ages, since it could not be justly established without their assent?

For my part, I see what things the clergy cannot obtain from the laity - not even an exemption from burying their dead almost under their altars.

Thus, I cannot easily believe that the laity should suffer themselves to be injuriously, and by force, deprived of any such great part of their rights.

I rather believe that this custom was instituted for some reasonable causes and with the consent of the laity.

What amazes me most is that Luther should be so angry and passionate for having one kind taken away from the laity in Communion, while he is not at all moved that children should be debarred from both!

He cannot deny that it was customary for children to receive Communion in the early times.

Although Christ said, '*Drink ye all of this*', (Matt. 26:27) this custom, if it was justly omitted, was undoubtedly done for very good reasons, although nobody may remember them.

Why, then, should we not think that the early custom of the laity's receiving the Sacrament in both kinds was taken away as well for good and just reasons, unknown at this time, which were perhaps not continued for any considerable time?

Moreover, if Luther examines the strict form of the Gospel narration, and leaves nothing in this matter to the Church, why does he not command that the Sacrament should always be received at supper-time, or rather after it? [18]

Finally, in the manner of receiving this Sacrament, it should be deemed more appropriate to do what ought to be done.

If the whole Church does wrong in the custom of denying the laity Communion under the form of wine, with what reason does Luther dare put water in the wine?

I do not think that he is so bold as to consecrate without water. For he has no example in Our Lord's Supper, not a certain one, of the Apostles' Tradition of mingling water with the wine: He learned it only by the custom of the Church.

If he thinks himself obliged to be obedient to the custom of the Church in this part, why does he so arrogantly oppose Her in the other?

Whatever Luther may chatter concerning this matter, for my part I judge it safer to believe that the laity does rightly communicate, though under one kind, rather than to believe that the clergy for so many ages were damned, for omitting both, as he contends.

For he calls them all wicked, *'and so wicked, that they all were guilty of the crime of Gospel Treason. If,* (says he) *we must name them that are heretics and schismatics; it is not the Bohemians, or Grecians, for they endeavour to follow the Gospel, but the Romans who are the heretics and schismatics, and, by their fictions, presume against the evident truth of Scripture'.*

If Luther admits nothing else but the evident and plain text of Scripture, why does he not command the Eucharist to be received at supper-time, as I have pointed out?

The Scriptures mention that Christ did so. Luther would have much better reasons to believe that this institution of the Church - giving Communion to the laity under one kind - was done by the authority of God.

---

[18] Jesus instituted the Eucharist on Holy Thursday *"the night on which he was betrayed"* (1 Corinthians 11:23), as he celebrated the Last Supper with his apostles (*Compendium*, Number 272).

It was not instituted by any human invention but by God's authority; and it should be received when the people are fasting.

As St. Augustine says, *'it has pleased the Holy Ghost that the Body of our Lord, which by the Apostles was received after other food, should in the Church be received fasting, before any other food'*.

It is very probable that the Holy Ghost, who governs the Church of Christ, just as He has changed the time of receiving the Sacrament from supper to the morning, while fasting, has also changed the laity's receiving under both, to the communicating under one kind.

If He could change the one, why could He not alter the other one also?

Luther shows plainly in this place, that his intention is to flatter the Bohemians, whose perfidy he previously detested.

None of those, whom he calls papists and flatterers of the Pope, do so much flatter the Roman Prelates as Luther flatters the very scum of the Bohemian common people.

He is not without reason indeed: for he foresees that the Germans, whom he formerly deceived under the form of a simple sheep, would reject him, as soon as they should perceive him to be a devouring wolf.

Therefore, he insinuates himself into the esteem of the Bohemians, and, as much as he is able to, makes himself friends of the Mammon of iniquity (Lk. 16:9).

Thus, since he has already entered into their errors, he may also pass into their country when he is banished from his own.

In order that some remarkable action may make him more commendable to them when he goes, he endeavours to extinguish all the force and authority of ecclesiastical customs, so that, in the end, if his designs should succeed, he would bring all such customs to ruin - which God forbid!

Luther aims at greater things than he can expect to accomplish. Therefore, he pleads for the laity, though his thoughts are quite contrary to what he pretends them to be: he sweetly offers them bread with one hand, and holds a scourge for them in the other (Lk. 11:11).

Thus, in the first place, he is altogether for the laity being admitted to receive Communion under both kinds. In so doing, wouldn't one naturally think that he endeavours to increase their devotion towards the Sacrament?

But look a little further at what he intends: at last he brings his business so far as to desire that there ought to be no obligation to receive at Easter, and that no time may be appointed to them for receiving.

Every man should be left to his own discretion.

Nay, further still, Luther proposes *'that none should receive more than once in his whole life and only at the day of his death'*.

Now death is uncertain, and at that time, many are not able to receive it.

So he, that pretended to stand for the people receiving Communion under both kinds, recommends quite the contrary, that is, that *'it may be lawful for them never to receive under any kind'*.

And he esteems it to be an excellent *liberty* that the people may be altogether freed from receiving the Sacrament at all.

Wherefore, though this serpent seems to flatter you with an amiable countenance, his venomous tail seeks to sting you.

He makes it quite manifest that he is more concerned about the people's receiving under one kind, than about their abstaining from both.

And even as the old serpent - being cast out of heaven - envied man's happiness in paradise, so Luther, being fallen by his own sin, under the penalty of excommunication - and thereby deprived of the wholesome and life-giving Communion under both kinds - endeavours to entrap all others in the same snare.

Thus, by being freed from the obligation of receiving under both kinds, he hopes they may, little by little, receive under no kind at all.

The further you advance in reading his libel, the more you will discover this detestable trick of his.

About Transubstantiation

THE CHURCH FORBIDS any man to believe that the true bread and true wine remain after Consecration. [19]
Luther makes this prohibition a second captivity.
Thus, contrary to the belief of the whole Christian world, both now and for so many ages past, Luther endeavours to persuade us

---

[19] Jesus Christ is present in the Eucharist in a unique and incomparable way. He is present in a true, real and substantial way, with his Body and his Blood, with his Soul and his Divinity. In the Eucharist, therefore, there is present in a sacramental way, that is, under the Eucharistic species of bread and wine, Christ whole and entire, God and Man (*Compendium*, Number 282).

that the Body and Blood of Christ are in the Eucharist in such a manner that the substance of true bread and true wine remains after Consecration.

I suppose that afterwards, when it pleases him, he will deny the substance of the Body and Blood to be there, when he has a mind to change his opinion - as he has already done three times.

And yet he feigns that he teaches those things moved with pity towards the captivity of the *Israelites* in which they are kept slaves to *Babylon*.

Thus he calls the whole Church, *Babylon*, and the faith of Christ, *slavery*.

And this *merciful man* offers liberty to all those who will sever themselves from the Church and become corrupted with the infection of this rotten and separated member.

But it is worth our while to know by what means he invites people to this more than servile liberty.

He regards this to be his greatest and principal reason:

'*Scripture is not to be forced, either by men or angels; but to be kept in the simplest signification that can be, and unless required by some manifest circumstances, it is not to be taken otherwise than in its proper and grammatical sense; lest occasion Scriptures.*

'But - he also says - *the Divine Words are forced, if that which Christ called 'bread', be taken for the accidents of bread; and what he called 'wine', for the form of wine.*

'*Therefore, by all means, the true bread and true wine remain upon the altar, lest violence be done to Christ's words, if the species be taken for the substance.*

'Because, - he continues - *seeing that the Evangelists write so plainly, that Christ took bread, and blessed it; and afterwards, in the Book of the Acts, and by Paul, it is called 'bread', we ought to take it for true bread, and true wine, as a true chalice. Because they do not say themselves that the chalice is transubstantiated'.*

This is Luther's great and, as he says, chief reason, which I hope to handle so as to give all men to understand of how little consequence it is.

In the first place, although the Evangelists had plainly said what Luther says they did, nothing is clearly proved for Luther.

On the contrary, they say nothing in any place that may seem to favour his side.

'*Do they not write* (says he) *that He took bread, and blessed it?*'

What does that argue? We confess He took bread, and blessed it; but we flatly deny that he gave bread to his disciples, after he had made it his Body.

The Evangelists do not say He did thus.

So that this may be made more evidently manifest, and that there may be less room left for wrangling, let us hear the Evangelists themselves.

St. Mathew's words are these:

'And whilst they were at supper, Jesus took bread and blessed and broke and gave to his disciples and said: Take ye and eat. **This is my body**. *And taking the chalice, he gave thanks and gave to them, saying: Drink ye all of this. For* **this is my blood** *of the new testament, which shall be shed for many unto remission of sins'* (Matt. 26:26-28).

St. Mark's words are these, *'and whilst they were eating, Jesus took bread; and blessing, broke and gave to them and said: Take ye.* **This is my body**. *And having taken the chalice, giving thanks, he gave it to them. And they all drank of it. And he said to them:* **This is my blood of the New Testament**, *which shall be shed for many'* (Mk. 14:22-24).

St. Luke has it after this manner: *'and taking bread, he gave thanks and broke and gave to them, saying:* **This is my body**, *which is given for you. Do this for a commemoration of me. In like manner, the chalice also, after he had supped, saying:* **This is the chalice, the New Testament in my blood**, *which shall be shed for you'* (Lk. 22:19-20).

In all these words of the Evangelists, I see none where, after the Consecration, the Sacrament is called 'bread' and 'wine', but only 'Body' and 'Blood.'

They say that Christ took bread in his hands, which we all confess; however, when the Apostles received it, was not called 'bread' but 'Body.'

Yet Luther endeavours to rest the words of the Gospel by his own interpretation. *'Take, eat; this',* that is, *'this bread'* (he says, which He had taken and broken,) *is my Body.'*

This is Luther's interpretation, not Christ's words, nor the sense of His words. [20]

---

[20] Sacred Scripture must be read and interpreted with the help of the Holy Spirit and under the guidance of the Magisterium of the Church according to three criteria: 1) it must be read with attention to the content and unity of the whole of Scripture; 2) it must be read within the living Tradition of the Church; 3) it must be read with attention to the analogy of faith, that is, the inner harmony which exists among the truths of the faith themselves (*Compendium*, Number 19).

If He had given to His disciples the bread which He took, without converting it into His Flesh, before He gave it to them, bidding them 'take and eat'; then it had been rightly said that He gave what He took in His hands; for then He had given nothing else but bread.

But seeing that He turned the bread into His Flesh before He gave it to the Apostles to eat, they now received not the bread that He took, but His Body into which He had turned the bread. [21]

If someone took a seed and gave to another the flower sprung from it, he would not give what he had taken, even though the common course of nature had made the one out of the other.

So, likewise, Christ gave the Apostles what he took in His hand, when He turned the bread into His own Body, by so great a miracle.

Unless, perhaps some will say that when Aaron took a rod in his hand and cast it from him (Ex 7:12), the substance of the rod remained with the serpent, and the serpent's substance with the rod, when it was restored again.

If the rod could not remain with the serpent, how much less can the bread remain with the Flesh of Christ, that incomparable Substance?

Luther argues, or rather trifles, to show how simplistic his own faith is. Concerning the wine, Christ does not say, *'Hoc est Sanguis Meus'* but, *'Hic est Sanguis Meus.'*

I wonder why it should enter into any man's mind to write thus: for who does not see that this makes nothing at all for Luther's argument, but rather, it makes against him?

It had seemed more for his purpose, if Christ had said, *'Hoc est Sanguis Meus,'* because then Luther might have had some colour at least, whereby he might have referred the demonstrative article to the wine.

Although 'wine' is of the neuter gender, Christ did not say *'Hoc'* but *'Hic est Sanguis Meus.'* Although 'bread' is of the masculine gender, He says *'Hoc est Corpus Meum'*, not *'Hic'*, that it may appear, by both articles, that He did not mean to give either bread or wine, but His own Body and Blood.

---

[21] After he had gathered with his apostles in the Cenacle, Jesus took bread in his hands. He broke it and gave it to them saying, *"Take this and eat it, all of you; this is my Body which will be given up for you"*. Then, he took the cup of wine in his hands and said, *"Take this and drink of this, all of you. This is the cup of my Blood, the Blood of the new and everlasting covenant. It will be shed for you and for all so that sins may be forgive. Do this in memory of me"* (*Compendium*, Number 273).

Is it not very ridiculous that Luther should imagine this pronoun *Hoc* not to be intended by Christ to refer to His Body?

It is thus only for the convenience of the Greek and Latin tongues, and therefore we are sent back to the Hebrew.

Since Hebrew does not have the neuter gender, it is obvious that it cannot declare what Christ referred to in the same way Greek or Latin can.

In the Hebrew, the article should be of the masculine gender, that is, *'Hic est Corpus Meum'*. Nevertheless, the matter would still be doubtful because that phrase might seem forced by the necessity of the Hebrew language, having no neuter gender.

But because 'bread' and 'body' are of different genders in Latin, the translator from the Greek should have joined the article with *Panis* (bread), if he had not found that the Gospel demonstration was made of the Body.

Moreover, when Luther confesses that the same difference of gender exists in Greek, he might easily know that when the Evangelists wrote in Greek - if they had not known our Lord's Mind - they would have put in the article relating to the 'bread.'

But, by the article relating to the 'Body' the Evangelists were willing to teach the Christians that Christ did not give bread to His disciples in Communion, but His Body.

Wherefore, when Luther - to serve his own interests - interprets the words of Christ *'Take, and eat, this is My Body'* referring to the bread He had taken, it is not I but it is Christ Himself Who teaches us to understand the contrary, if the Evangelists have rightly delivered to us His words.

What Christ gave them did seem to be bread, but it was not bread; it was His own Body.

Otherwise He should say not *'Hoc'*, that it might be expounded for *'Hic'*, but, more properly *'Hic Panis est Corpus Meum'*.

By this saying He might teach His disciples what Luther now teaches to the whole Church, which is, *'that in the Eucharist the Body of Christ and the bread are together.'*

On the contrary, Our Saviour spoke in that manner that He might more clearly manifest that only His Body is in the Sacrament, not bread.

How magnificently Luther brings this in for his argument, *'that Christ speaks of the chalice, which nobody holds to be transubstantiated.'*

It amazes me that the man is not ashamed of so vast a folly.

When Christ says, *'this chalice of the New Testament is My Blood'*, what does that achieve for Luther?

What else does it signify, except that what He gave His disciples to drink was His own Blood?

By those words of Christ, will Luther make it appear that the substance of wine remains because Christ speaks of Blood?

Or is it that the wine cannot be changed into Blood because the chalice is still there?

I wish he had chosen for himself some other matter in which he might have played and sported with less danger.

Luther excuses the Bohemians and Greeks from heresy so much that he calls all the Roman Catholics heretics.

In so doing, he shows himself to be a worse heretic than either of them.

He not only denies the Faith that the whole Church believes, but also persuades people to believe worse than the Greeks or Bohemians ever did.

I have so far disputed these things so that I might make clear that what Luther contends cannot be confirmed by the words of Christ and the Evangelists. Nay, quite the contrary is very clear in their sayings: bread is not in the Eucharist.

Luther says that in the Acts of the Apostles the Eucharist is called bread. I wish he would show us the place.

For my part, I find nothing that is ambiguous and that seems to speak of a common banquet rather than the Sacrament.

Yet I admit that the Apostle speaks more than once of bread, following the custom of Scripture, which sometimes calls a thing not by its name but what it was before.

For instance, when it says, *'and they every one cast down their rods, and they were turned into serpents: but Aaron's rod devoured their rods'* (Ex. 7:12) they were no longer rods, but serpents.

Or else perhaps Saint Paul was content to call it what it appeared to be judging it sufficient to feed the people with milk (Heb. 5:12), who were as yet inexpert in the Faith.

Thus, they demanded nothing of them at first, except to believe that the Body of Christ was, in some manner, present in the Sacrament.

Afterwards, little by little, they would feed them with more solid food as they gathered more strength in Christ.

Luther might have also touched on that place in the Acts of the Apostles where St. Peter, while speaking to the people, was imparting to them the Faith of Christ.

Peter did not dare as yet say anything openly of Christ's Divinity, so cautious were the Apostles then of rashly exposing the sacred mysteries to the people.

When Christ first instituted the Blessed Sacrament, He had no difficulty in teaching His Apostles - whom He had for so long instructed in His own doctrine - that the substance of bread and wine no longer remained in the Sacrament.

While the forms of both remained, the substance was changed into His Body and Blood.

This He taught so plainly that it is very strange that anybody should ever afterwards question a thing so clear in itself.

How could He have more adequately said that no bread and wine remain in the Sacrament, when He said, *'this is My Body?'*

He did not say, *'My Body is in this'*, or, 'with this which you see, is My Body', as if it should consist in the bread, or with the bread.

On the contrary, when He said *'this is My Body'*, He manifestly declared that what He then gave was His Body, thus shutting the mouth of every yelping fellow.

By His Will, Christ changed bread into His Body. Even though He had called *'bread'* what He gave to the Apostles - which He did not - yet His teaching to those who were present was that what He called *'bread'* was none other than His Body, into which the bread was changed by His Will.

Nobody, then, could doubt what Christ wanted us understand by the name of bread.

That very circumstance - because Luther does admit circumstances - evidently shows that the word *bread*, when turned into Flesh, signifies the species and not the substance of bread. And this is so without doing any violence to the texts.

Unless Luther sticks so closely to the propriety of words as to believe that, in heaven, Christ was wheaten or barley bread because He says of Himself, *'I am the living bread which came down from heaven'* (John 6:41).

Or that He was a vine laden with real grapes because He said, *'I am the true vine: and my Father is the husbandman'* (John 15:1).

Or that the Elect shall be rewarded in heaven with corporal pleasures, because Christ said, *'I dispose to you, as My Father hath disposed to Me, a kingdom, That you may eat and drink at My table, in My kingdom: and may sit upon thrones, judging the twelve tribes of Israel'* (Lk. 22:29-30)?

Luther takes a great deal of pain to confute the arguments of the *Neoteries*, who, out of Aristotle's school, endeavoured to maintain and prove Transubstantiation by philosophical reasons,.

Here he troubles himself more than is required. The Church does not believe in Transubstantiation because the *Neoteries* disputed it, but rather because She believed it from the beginning and taught that all should believe it also, so that none should be confused.

They therefore exercise their wit with philosophical reasons in order to teach that no absurd consequence can follow the belief that the change of bread into a new substance does not necessarily leave, but take away the former.

Luther says, *'this doctrine of Transubstantiation is risen in the Church within these three hundred years; whereas before, for above twelve hundred years, from Christ's birth, the Church had true faith.*

Yet all this while there was no mention made of this prodigious (as he calls it) *word 'Transubstantiation'.'*

If he strives thus only about the word Transubstantiation, I suppose none will trouble him to believe in it.

But if he will believe that the bread is changed into the Flesh and the wine into the Blood and that nothing remains of the bread and wine but the species - this is, in one word, the meaning of those who put in the word *Transubstantiation.* [22]

Suppose that no one had ever thought of the word before but the Ancients believed in the doctrine. Then the Church, although for the first time, taught it to be true.

Why shouldn't Luther be obedient to the present teaching of the whole Church, persuaded that what was previously unknown, is now revealed at length to the Church?

For as the Spirit inspires where He is willing (John 3:8), so likewise He inspires when He pleases.

But this is not the case at all, as Luther feigns, when he says that *'this doctrine of Transubstantiation is risen up within three hundred years.'*

Yet let it not vex him to allow us four hundred years; because I think it is that many since Hugo de Saint-Victor wrote a book of the

---

[22] Transubstantiation means the change of the whole substance of bread into the substance of the Body of Christ and of the whole substance of wine into the substance of his Blood. This change is brought about in the Eucharistic prayer through the efficacy of the word of Christ and by the action of the Holy Spirit. However, the outward characteristics of bread and wine, that is the "Eucharistic species", remain unaltered (*Compendium*, Number 283).

Sacraments, in which the sense of his words you may find to be of the same effect, though he did not use the word Transubstantiation itself.

'Though this Sacrament (he says) *is but one, yet three different things are proposed in it; namely, the visible form, the Real Presence of the Body and virtue of spiritual Grace.'*

You see how he records the accidents of bread, not the substance; and the true substance of the Body, nor the form.

And more plainly a little further: *'for what we see is the species of the bread and wine; but what we believe to be under that form is the very Body of Christ which hung on the Cross, and the very Blood which flowed from His side.'*

He is yet clearer in another place, where he says, *'by the word of sanctification, the true substance of bread and wine is turned, or changed into the true Body and Blood of Christ, only the form of bread and wine remaining, and the substance passing into another substance.'*

By this, then, it appears that this doctrine of Transubstantiation is *somewhat* more ancient than Luther pretends it to be.

But, to better confirm this, we will show that what he thinks to have been invented within the past three hundred years was indeed the Faith of the holy Fathers over a thousand years ago.

It is certain that the faithful, for over a thousand years past, believed the substance of bread and wine to be truly changed into the Body and Blood of Jesus Christ.

It amazes me to see that Luther is not ashamed of himself when he says that this belief of Transubstantiation has not been in the Church for more than three hundred years.

Who does not know that Eusebius Emissenus died over six hundred years ago?

He, as if dreading the proclamation of such false opinions, said, *'let all doubt or ambiguity of unfaithfulness be put away: for He who is the Author of the Gift, is also the Witness of the Truth.*

'The invisible Priest converts the visible creatures into His own Body and Blood by His veiled power, saying; 'take and eat, this is My Body'.'

Doesn't this holy man say most plainly that the substance of bread and wine is changed into the substance of the Body and Blood?

What could be said more to the purpose, than this of St. Augustine?

'We honour (he says) *invisible things, that is, the Flesh and Blood in the visible form of bread and wine.'*

He does not say, *in* the bread and wine, but *in the form of* bread and wine.

Luther denies that the form of bread is to be called 'bread'. Does he think that St. Augustine should name the form of bread, which is the true substance of bread?

Likewise St. Gregory of Nyssa says, *'that before the Consecration, it is but bread; but when it is consecrated by mystery, it is made, and called, the Body of Christ.'*

His saying that it is bread before the Consecration leads us to understand that it is not bread after the Consecration.

Theophilus also, expounding on the words, *'Hoc est'* etc., *'this is My Body'*, etc. says, *'this, which now I give, and you receive. Because the bread is not only a figure of the Body of Christ, but is changed into the proper Body of the Flesh and Blood of Christ.'*

And a while after he says, *'if we did see the Flesh and Blood of Christ, we could not endure to eat them. Therefore our Lord, condescending to our weakness, preserves the forms of the bread and wine; but changes the bread and wine into His own true Flesh and Blood.'*

Here Luther is beaten down twice by this good and learned man.

First, because he teaches that the article *'Hoc'* is not to be understood as Luther interprets it.

Hoc, that is, *Hic Panis*; but *Hoc*, that is, this which now I give, My Body, and you take.

Secondly, he plainly says that the form of the bread and wine remains, and that the substance is changed into the Body and Blood.

But what else do they mean, they who use the word *Transubstantiation*, than what Theophilus said?

And, since he was dead a hundred years before the word *Transubstantiation* was ever used, it was not within three hundred years, as Luther feigns.

What need do I have to mention St. Cyril, who, not only affirms the same thing, but almost in the same words?

'For God, (he says) *condescending to our frailties, lest we should abhor Flesh and Blood on the holy altars, infuses the force of life into what is offered, by changing them into the truth of His own proper Flesh.'*

What I have related above fully and plainly demonstrates that the ancient Fathers did not believe the Body of Christ to be in the Eucharist in such a manner as though the bread should still remain.

Also, what I have previously quoted from St. Ambrose, when he said, *'that although the form of bread and wine is seen, nevertheless we are to believe that there is nothing else after the Consecration, but the Body and Blood of Christ.'*

You see how the Holy Father says, *'that it is not only the Body and Blood, but that there is nothing besides them, although the bread and wine seem to be there.'*

And St Ambrose taught this more than a thousand years ago, and not within the past three hundred years, as Luther feigns that this belief of Transubstantiation has been raised.

Neither can I believe that any of the ancient Fathers would have approved that fine comparison of Luther's, that is, of iron joined with fire.

For nobody ever said that iron is so converted into fire that only its form remains, and its substance is changed into that of fire, which was the belief of all the Ancients concerning bread and the Flesh of Christ.

If, perhaps, an individual had held a contrary view, still *one swallow makes no summer*. And that man, whoever he was, should be excused rather than imitated, for not perfectly seeing through a matter not in dispute at that time.

If such a man were good and alive, undoubtedly he would not argue against a matter contrary to the belief of the rest of the Church and of so many ages.

Having so much esteem for the Body of Christ, as he ought to have, he would see that there is no substance worthy to be mixed with that Substance which created all substances.

Thus, he will more easily agree that any two other substances could remain together, rather than that any thing remain mixed with the adorable Body of Christ.

Moreover, I suppose that the early Fathers would give little approval to that comparison of Luther, whereby he intends to prove that the bread remains with the Flesh as God did remain with man in the Person of Christ.

The most learned and the most holy of the ancient Fathers declare in various places that the bread is changed into Flesh.

None of them was so wicked or ignorant as to think that the Humanity was changed into the Divinity.

Unless, perhaps, Luther will devise a new Person: so that, as God took on Himself the nature of man, so God and man take on the nature of bread and wine.

If he believes this, he shall be accounted a heretic by all those who are not heretics.

Wherefore, to conclude this discourse on Transubstantiation, it is evident that the present Faith of the Church is true, which teaches that the substance of bread or wine does not remain in the Eucharist. And this is evidenced by Christ's words and by the judgment of the holy Fathers.

Whence it follows that, by teaching the contrary, Luther's belief is false and heretical.

From this persuasion, I am amazed at what advantage he promises the people: *'is it that nobody should consider himself a heretic, if perhaps he should be of his opinion?'*

Luther himself confesses that there is no harm in believing as the Catholic Church now believes. But on the contrary, the whole Church condemns those who are of Luther's opinion to be heretics.

Therefore, he ought not to persuade anyone whom he wishes well to be of his judgment, as it is condemned by the whole Church.

Rather, Luther should advise those he loves to believe what the Church teaches.

Thus, that opinion of Luther is false, since it is against the public Faith, not only of this time, but also of all ages. He does not free from captivity those who believe him.

Instead, in drawing them away from the liberty of Faith - which he himself confesses to be a safe hold - he takes them captive, leading them into a precipice, into inaccessible, uncertain, doubtful and dangerous ways. *'He that loveth danger shall perish in it'* (Ecclus. 3:27).

The Mass is a Good Work

 HIS MAN - WHO is *'free from any evil'* - has escaped these two captivities, which he imagines to himself.
Now, so that he may not let his mind be captive to the obedience of God, he overcomes a third captivity, as he pretends, and proposes a liberty whereby he may captivate the whole Church.

This worse-than-sacrilegious caitiff endeavours to scatter abroad the Church's most splendid congregation; to extinguish its Pillar of Fire; to violate the Ark of the Covenant; and to destroy the chief and only Sacrifice which reconciles us to God, which is always offered for the sins of the people.

Inasmuch as in him lies, he robs the Mass of all the benefits that flow from it to the people. [23]

He denies that the Mass is a good work, or that it brings to the people any kind of benefit.

Here I do not know what should amaze us more: his wickedness, his foolish hope, or his mad pride.

Luther, seeing so many obstructions before him, as he himself mentions, offers nothing to remove the least of them.

Instead, it seems that he attempts to pierce a rock with a reed.

He himself sees and confesses that the beliefs of the holy Fathers are against him, as well as the Canon of the Mass and the custom of the universal Church, confirmed as it is by the practice of so many ages and by the consent of so many people.

What defence, then, does he present against so innumerable, so powerful and so invincible armies?

His customary force rages: he strives to breed discord, move seditions, and excite the common people against the nobility.

And, in order that he may more easily stir them up to a revolt, by his foolish and weak policy, he falsely pretends that he has Christ for Captain of the whole army in the camp, and that the trumpet of the Gospel sounds only for him.

This is the most ridiculous stratagem that was ever invented.

What living man is so wicked or blockish as to think that the Church, the mystical Body of Christ, should be dilacerated in such manner, that the Head be severed from the rest of the members, which still remain joined together? [24]

---

[23] [The Eucharist] is the source and summit of all Christian life. In the Eucharist, the sanctifying action of God in our regard and our worship of him reach their high point. It contains the whole spiritual good of the Church, Christ himself, our Pasch. Communion with divine life and the unity of the People of God are both expressed and effected by the Eucharist. Through the Eucharistic celebration we are united already with the liturgy of heaven and we have a foretaste of eternal life (*Compendium*, Number 274).

[24] Christ "*is the Head of the body, the Church*" (Colossians 1:18). The Church lives from him, in him and for him. Christ and the Church make up the "whole Christ" (Saint Augustine); "Head and members form, as it were, one and the same mystical person" (Saint Thomas Aquinas) – (*Compendium*, Number 157).

Or that Christ, Who never abandoned the Flesh that He once took, should cast off the Church, for whose sake He took that Flesh?[25]

Would He absent Himself from the Church for so many ages, His Church, with whom He promised to remain to the end of the world and now pass to Luther's side, he who is Her professed enemy?

But, pray, let us see by what enchantment he attempts to prove that, in truth, Christ is on his side, as he brags.

After many idle circumstances, he goes about to define what the Mass is.

Afterwards, he separates the ceremonies of the Mass from the Mass itself.

Then, he examines the Lord's Supper, and ponders the words which Christ used in the institution of the Sacrament of the Mass.

Having found in them the word *Testament*, as if it were something very obscure, he begins to triumph as though he had conquered his enemies.

He beautifies with words this new found *mystery* of his, as he calls it.

And, as if it had never been heard of before, he teaches us, with greatest gravity, what a Testament is.

He bawls aloud that *'it is to be marked and taken notice of that a Testament is the promise of a dying person, by which he bequeaths the inheritance, and institutes heirs.*

'Therefore, (says he) *this Sacrament of the Mass is nothing other than the Testament of Christ.*

'And the Testament is nothing but the promise of the eternal heritage giving His Body and Blood to us Christians, whom He appointed for His heirs, as a sign for the ratification of His promise.'

This he repeats over and over again; he inculcates, and fixes it, intending to make it his immoveable foundation whereon to build wood, hay and stubble (1 Cor. 3:12).

Thus, by laying this ground-work – *'that the Mass is the Testament of Christ'* - he boasts that he will destroy all the wickedness that impious men have brought into the Sacrament, as he says, and he will clearly prove that we ought to receive Communion with Faith alone, without much regard to any type of good works whatsoever.

---

[25] God *"desires all men to be saved and to come to the knowledge of the truth"* (1 Timothy 2:4), that is, of Jesus Christ. For this reason, Christ must be proclaimed to all according to his own command, *"Go forth and teach all nations"* (Matthew 28:19). And this is brought about by Apostolic Tradition (*Compendium*, Number 11).

Accordingly, the more in the wrong our consciences are and the more moved with the sting or titillation of our sins, the holier is our state for approach Holy Communion. [26]

Again, the clearer, purer and freer our consciences are from the stain of sin, the worse is our capacity in which to receive Communion. [27]

'Further, (says he) Mass is no sacrifice; it is only profitable to the priest, not to the people; it avails nothing either to the dead or the living; to sing Mass for sins, for any necessity, or for the dead is an impious error; fraternities, as also the annual commemorations for the dead, are vain and wicked things; our voluntary maintaining of priests, monks, canons, brothers, and whatsoever we call religious, is to be abolished.'

These, therefore, with many other great, good things, he glories to have found out by this discovery: *the Blessed Sacrament is the Testament of Christ.*

And now he inveighs against the *sententious Doctors* - as he calls them. He exclaims against all who preach to the people:

'Those who write and preach so much in defence of the Blessed Sacrament of the Eucharist - of whom none says anything regarding the Testament - most impiously conceal that incomparable good from the people, which so long since might have been beneficially known.

'The laity, (says he) neither alive, nor after death, will ever receive any benefit by the Mass.'

Because of his ignorance of the subject, he denounces all priests and monks of this day in the world, with their bishops and superiors as idolaters, and to be in a very dangerous condition.

I do not discuss how true that *mystery* of Luther is - in applying so *accurately* his definition of Testament to the Sacrament - from which he attributes so much glory to himself.

---

[26] To receive Holy Communion one must be fully incorporated into the Catholic Church and be in the state of grace, that is, not conscious of being in mortal sin. Anyone who is conscious of having committed a grave sin must first receive the sacrament of Reconciliation before going to Communion. (*Compendium*, Number 291).

[27] Sin is "a word, an act, or a desire contrary to the eternal Law" (Saint Augustine). It is an offence against God in disobedience to his love. It wounds human nature and injures human solidarity. Christ in his passion fully revealed the seriousness of sin and overcame it with his mercy (*Compendium*, Number 392).

At the same time, I do not see why he should brag so much of this new invention of his.

Indeed, I do not know who he hears preach or where he is; but here, I am sure, we have heard preachers, over and over again, who treat of those things which Luther brings out as being so new and exquisite:

'That Christ is a Testator; that He made His Testament in the Last Supper; that He promised an inheritance, which He declared to be the Kingdom of Heaven; that He instituted the faithful for His heirs; that the Sacrament is a holy sign exhibited for a seal.'

Not only these and such like, but also *'the number of witnesses, the bill, and other rites of testaments they unfolded to us out of the deepest secrets of both Laws, and applied all of them exactly to the Sacrament.'*

This they did more consciously and truly than Luther, because they referred to the same Testament; not only what Christ did at His Last Supper, but also what He suffered on the Cross.

They differ from Luther only in this: they did not find out the admirable and hitherto unheard-of *'benefits'* of the Mass: the clergy loses all its fruits in this life, and the laity in the life to come.

The people would not keep the clergy saying Mass, if they were persuaded that they could reap no spiritual good from it.

It is worth our while to see from what tree Luther gathers this fruit.

He has very often repeated that the Sacrament of the Eucharist is the sign of the Testament, and the Testament is nothing else but the promise of inheritance.

From this, he thinks that, as a consequence, it follows that the Mass cannot be a good work, or a sacrifice.

If anyone agrees with this, he must immediately admit that catalogue of plagues whereby Luther endeavours to confound the whole face of the Church.

But if you deny it, then he can do nothing with so monstrous a design.

I am almost ashamed of the arguments whereby Luther pretends to teach these things. They are so trifling and frivolous in a matter of so great a majesty. Thus he concludes (for I will give you his own words):

'You have heard that Mass is nothing else but the divine promise, or testament of Christ, commended by the Sacrament of His Body and Blood; which, if it be true, you understand, that by any means it cannot be a work. Nor is it to be used after any other manner, than by Faith alone. And Faith is not a work, but the mistress and life of works.'

It is a strange thing, that, after so much painstaking, he vents nothing but mere wind.

Although he would have us believe his view to be of such strength as to overturn mountains, yet, it truly seems to me to lack enough force to shake a reed.

Like an ape in purple he embellishes this ridiculous matter. If you take away the covers of his words; if you take away the exclamations whereby he so often rails and insults like a conqueror - though not as yet entered the battle against the Church, nor clearly proved his opinion - you will find that nothing remains except a naked and miserable piece of sophistry.

What he has said by that heap of words is that Mass is a promise, and therefore not a work.

Who would not pity Luther, who is so blockish as not to realise his own impertinence?

Or, if he does realise it, who would not be shocked and offended by his thinking all Christians so dull in not discerning or comprehending such manifest follies?

I shall not dispute with him about the Testament or promise, or the whole definition, or its application to the Sacrament. I will not trouble him so much.

He may perhaps find others who will ruin the best part of his foundation, by saying, *'the Testament is the promise of the Gospel Law, as the Old Testament was of the Law of Moses'*, and by denying it to be rightly handled by Luther.

For neither was the Testator specific in naming what He left to the heir - or who He had appointed to be heir over all - nor is the remission of sins bequeathed as an inheritance in the same way as the Kingdom of Heaven.

The remission of sins is rather the way to heaven. [28]

If anyone should urge and press Luther in these and similar sayings, by fastening these engines in any part of his structure, perhaps he might shake its whole frame.

---

[28] The Eucharist is a pledge of future glory because it fills us with every grace and heavenly blessing. It fortifies us for our pilgrimage in this life and makes us long for eternal life. It unites us already to Christ seated at the right hand of the Father, to the Church in heaven and to the Blessed Virgin and all the saints (*Compendium*, Number 294).

But I shall leave that to someone who shall be willing to do it. And because Luther desires his foundation to remain unshaken, I shall not try to move it.

I will only show that the house he has built upon his foundation falls by itself.

To show this more plainly, let us briefly consider the origin of the matter, and examine the Mass by its first pattern.

Christ, in His most holy Supper in which He instituted this Sacrament, made His own Body and Blood of bread and wine and gave them to His disciples to be eaten and drunk.

A few hours afterwards, He offered the same Body and Blood on the Altar of the Cross, a Sacrifice to His Father for the sins of the people.

Once the sacrifice was finished, the Testament was consummated.

Being now near His death, He did, as some dying persons are wont to do, declare His will concerning what He desired to be done afterwards in commemoration of Him.

When He instituted the Sacrament, He gave His Body and Blood to His disciples and said, *'do this in commemoration of Me.'*

Anyone who diligently examines this will find Christ to be the eternal Priest Who instituted one Sacrifice, the greatest of all, the plenitude of all, as the sum of all others to be offered to God and given for food to the people.

He did so in place of all the sacrifices which were offered by the temporary priesthood of Moses. Law, in which there were many types and figures of this holy Sacrifice.

Thus, as Christ was the Priest, so His disciples represented the people for that time.

They themselves did not consecrate, but received the consecrated Sacrament from the hands of their Priest.

Shortly thereafter, God did elect and institute them priests, that they might consecrate the same Sacrament in commemoration of Him.

What else is this then, except that they should consecrate the Sacrament, give it to the people and offer it to God - not only receive it themselves?

However, if Luther argues that the priest cannot offer because Christ did not offer in His Supper, let him remember his own words, *'that a testament involves in it the death of the Testator.'*

Therefore, it has no force or power, nor is it in its full perfection, until the testator is dead.

Consequently, those things that Christ did first at His Supper and His Oblation on the Cross belong to the Testament.

On the Cross He consummated the Sacrifice which He began in the Supper. [29]

Therefore, as the Commemoration of the Consecration in the Supper and the Oblation on the Cross are celebrated and represented together in the Sacrament of the Mass, it is the death of Christ rather than the Supper that is more truly represented.

And so the Apostle, when writing to the Corinthians, *'as often as you shall eat this bread and drink the chalice'*, he adds, *'you shall show the death of the Lord'* not the *'Supper of our Lord'* (1 Cor. 11:26).

Let us now come to Luther's chief reasons whereby he argues that the Mass is neither a good work, nor a sacrifice.

Although it would be better to address the issue of sacrifice first, yet because he has first addressed the question of work, we will follow him.

He argues that the Mass is a promise, and therefore not a good work, because no promise is a work. We answer that the Mass that the priest celebrates cannot be called a promise any more appropriately than the Consecration of Christ can be called a promise.

Together we will demand of Luther: When Christ consecrated, did He not perform a work?

If he denies this - to wit, that Christ performed a work when He consecrated - we shall certainly begin to wonder why it is that when someone cuts an image out of wood, a work is done; but when Christ made Bread into His own Flesh, no work is done!

If Christ did perform any work, I am certain none will doubt that it was a good work.

Again, if the woman, who poured the ointment upon His Head (Matt. 26:7-10) did a good work, who doubts that He performed a good work,

---

[29] The Eucharist is a memorial in the sense that it makes present and actual the sacrifice which Christ offered to the Father on the cross, once and for all on behalf of mankind. The sacrificial character of the Holy Eucharist is manifested in the very words of institution, *"This is my Body which is given for you"* and *"This cup is the New Covenant in my Blood that will be shed for you"* (Luke 22:19-20). The sacrifice of the cross and the sacrifice of the Eucharist are one and the same sacrifice. The priest and the victim are the same; only the manner of offering is different: in a bloody manner on the cross, in an unbloody manner in the Eucharist (*Compendium*, Number 280).

when He gave His Body for our nourishment and offered it in Sacrifice to God?

If Christ's sacrificial work cannot be denied - unless by him who intends to trifle in so serious a matter - neither can it be denied that the priest works a good work in Mass.

In the Mass, the priest does nothing else but what Christ did in His Last Supper and on the Cross, for this is declared in Christ's own Words, *'do this in Commemoration of Me.'* [30]

By these words, what did He will that the Apostles represent and do in the Mass, except what He had done Himself in His Last Supper and on the Cross?

The Sacrament that He instituted and began at His Last Supper, He perfected on the Cross.

Precisely because water and blood did flow from the side of Christ dying on the Cross that water is mingled with the wine, according to the custom of the Church.

Since it cannot be denied that Christ did a good work in His Last Supper and on the Cross, neither can it be denied that the priest represents, and performs, the same things in the Mass.

How can then Luther pretend that the Mass is not a good work?

Luther so handles the matter as to say, *'because the communion of one layman does not profit another of the laity, so neither does the Mass of the priest profit the people.'*

How dim of sight is he, and how much does he endeavour to spread his darkness over the eyes of others, when he does not see that there is this difference in the case?

Now the laity receives out of the priest's hand as the Apostles first received from Christ's hands.

The priest performs now what Christ performed then, for he offers to God the same Body that was offered by Christ!

From whence also it appears how cold an argument is Luther's comparison of the Mass with the Sacrament of Baptism or Marriage.

He endeavours to prove that because one layman cannot be baptised for another, nor marry a wife for another man, so a priest cannot celebrate Mass for any other person!

---

[30] The celebrant of the Eucharist is a validly ordained priest (bishop or priest) who acts in the Person of Christ the Head and in the name of the Church (*Compendium*, Number 278).

He openly puts Marriage out of the number of the Sacraments, and Baptism too, in a sense, when he says, *'there is really but one Sacrament.'*

Why, then, does he now compare Baptism and Marriage with the Sacrament of the Mass, if he does not hold them to be Sacraments?

Even if Luther should confess that both of them are Sacraments - as indeed they are - neither of them are to be compared to the Sacrament of the Mass.

This Sacrament, which is the proper Body of Him who is Lord of all Sacraments, has a prerogative above all others, which He Himself made.

Since it is evident that the priest, in administering all other Sacraments, does good to all those who receive them, so in this Sacrament, while he offers it in the Mass, he also profits from it, and communicates good to all. [31]

Luther exacts with great severity that all Sacraments should be alike, having no difference among them, and that in the Sacrament of the Eucharist the priest's condition is no better than that of the laity.

Why, then, doesn't he compel the priest to receive Communion from the hands of another and not suffer him to take it himself, though he can consecrate it, just as he can not absolve himself, although he has the keys of Penance?

And what does he say about Faith, which he believes all men are to have in their own persons?

It is every man's own faith which profits him, not the priest's faith, even (says he) as *'Abraham has not believed for all the Jews.'*

I grant that this is very true, yet it proves no more than what it proposes; because, without every man's particular faith, Christ has not saved the people by offering Himself on the Cross.

Likewise, no one may think that the Mass of any priest should do it.

The Mass of every priest helps to salvation those who, by their faith, have deserved to be partakers of the greatest good communicated to many in the Mass. [32]

---

[31] In the sacraments the Church already receives a foretaste of eternal life, while *"awaiting in blessed hope, the appearing in glory of our great God and Saviour Christ Jesus"* (Titus 2:13) – (*Compendium*, Number 232).

[32] Faith is the supernatural virtue which is necessary for salvation. It is a free gift of God and is accessible to all who humbly seek it. The act of faith is a human act, that is, an act of the intellect of a person - prompted by the will moved by God - who freely assents to divine truth. Faith is also certain because it is founded on

Likewise, sometimes it may be advantageous to procure the infusion of faith into the faithless, as the Death and Passion of Christ did.

Thus, grace would be given to the Gentiles, whereby, through the hearing of the Word, they might come to the understanding of the Faith of Christ. [33]

the Word of God; it works *"through charity"* (Galatians 5:6); and it continually grows through listening to the Word of God and through prayer. It is, even now, a foretaste of the joys of heaven (*Compendium*, Number 28).

[33] Faith is the theological virtue by which we believe in God and all that he has revealed to us and that the Church proposes for our belief because God is Truth itself. By faith the human person freely commits himself to God. Therefore, the believer seeks to know and do the will of God because *"faith works through charity"* (Galatians 5:6) - (*Compendium*, Number 386).

The Sacrifice of the Mass

LUTHER EASILY REALISES that it is not difficult to destroy what he himself has built. Since the Mass can be a sacrifice or offering, which may be offered to God, he realises that it stands in his way and promises to remove this obstacle.

In order that he may more easily appear to do that, he objects against himself such things: *'and now,* (says he) *another, the greatest and most spacious of all scandals, which must be taken away; that is, the Mass, believed everywhere to be a sacrifice offered to God.'*

Now the words of the Canon seem to favour this view of sacrifice: *'these gifts, these presents and these holy sacrifices'*; and below that, *'this offering.'*

Likewise, he complains that the Mass is taken for a Sacrifice, etc., from thence Christ is called *'the Host of the Altar.'* [34]

To this may be added the words of the holy Fathers, so many examples, and the constant custom observed over the whole world.

You see, dear reader, what blocks he finds standing in his way: take notice with what Herculean strength he undertakes to remove them: to all these (says he) are to be constantly opposed the words and example of Christ.

But, pray, what words of Christ are these that have been unknown to so many holy Fathers in times past, and to the whole Church of Christ, during so many ages, and that now, like *a new Esdras*, Luther has discovered?

This he declares himself, when he says, *'for unless we bring it to pass - that the Mass be accounted a promise or testament - as the words clearly make out, we lose the whole Gospel and all comfort.'*

These are his words. It now remains that we see his example:

'Christ, (says he) *at His Last Supper, when He instituted this Sacrament and bequeathed the Testament, did not offer it to God the Father, nor performed it as a good work for others; but, sitting at the table, He proposed the same Testament, and exhibited a sign to every one of them.'*

Those are therefore *the Words of Christ*!?

Now at last, this is the example whereby Luther alone clearly sees that *the Mass is neither a Sacrifice nor an offering*!?

Is it not an amazing thing that, of so many holy Fathers, of so many eyes which have read the Gospel in the Church for so many ages, *none was ever so quick sighted as Luther to perceive something so evident*?

Furthermore, is it not amazing that at this present time, *they and we are all so blind* as not to discern what Luther brags to see so clearly, even though he points it out with his finger!

Isn't Luther rather mistaken in thinking to see something which, in reality, he does not see, or in endeavouring to show us something with his finger that is nowhere to be found?

Luther teaches that *'the Mass is no Sacrifice, because it is a promise.'*

Pray, what sort of proof is that, as if promise and sacrifice were as repugnant to one another as heat and cold?

---

[34] The altar is the symbol of Christ himself who is present both as sacrificial victim (the altar of the sacrifice) and as food from heaven which is given to us (the table of the Lord) – (Compendium, Number 288)

Now this reason of his is altogether so weak that it seems unworthy of an answer.

The many Sacrifices of Moses' Law were all figures of things to come, and yet they were promises in themselves, promising the things for which they were done. [35]

They were not only for the future, of which they were figures, but were also deliverances, expiations, purgations and purifications for the people then present, for whom they were solemnly offered every year.

This is so evident, that it leaves no plea for ignorance.

It makes Luther's dissimulation appear altogether ridiculous, when he argues that this cannot be done.

For not only he himself knows it, but all the people also know that they have been so often performed.

Now we come to the example of Christ, whereby Luther thinks he so vehemently oppresses us: according to him, *'Christ, in His Last Supper, neither used the Sacrament for a sacrifice, nor offered it to His Father'.*

From this, Luther goes about to prove that *'the Mass cannot be a Sacrifice or Offering for it ought to agree with the example of Christ, by Whom it was instituted.'*

Luther rigidly turns us to the example of Our Lord's Supper, which (says he) does not permit the priest to do anything that we do not read Christ to have done in it.

Therefore, the priests themselves must never receive the Sacrament which they consecrate because we do not read in the Gospel - where the Last Supper of Our Lord is narrated - that Our Lord received His own Body.

Although some Doctors and the whole Church do hold that He did receive it, yet that means nothing to Luther.

He discredits not only all the Doctors but the Faith of the whole Church, thinking that nothing should be believed except for what is

---

[35] The Eucharist was foreshadowed in the Old Covenant above all in the annual Passover meal celebrated every year by the Jews with unleavened bread to commemorate their hasty, liberating departure from Egypt. Jesus foretold it in his teaching and he instituted it when he celebrated the Last Supper with his apostles in a Passover meal. The Church, faithful to the command of her Lord, *"Do this in memory of me"* (1 Corinthians 11:24), has always celebrated the Eucharist, especially on Sunday, the day of the Resurrection of Jesus (*Compendium*, Number 276).

clearly confirmed by the Scriptures – as he writes in the Sacrament of Orders.

In this sort of Scripture, I believe that he will not find that Christ received His own Body at His Last Supper.

Whence it follows then, as I have said, that if Luther binds us so strictly to the example of the Last Supper, the priests ought not to consume what they themselves consecrate.

If then Luther allows the priests to receive, because the Apostles received - and they are commanded to do what the Apostles did, not what Christ did - then the priests must never consecrate, because it was Christ who consecrated, and not the Apostles.

From the foregoing, it is clearly shown that the priests do not only perform what Christ did in His Last Supper, but also what He afterwards did on the Cross. [36]

The Apostles left us some things by Tradition, which Christ either never did or which we do not read that He had done, i.e., most of the ceremonies and signs used in the Consecration are, I believe, delivered down to us from the Apostles themselves.

Furthermore, they repeat some words in the Canon of the Mass as if said by Christ Himself, which are not read in Scripture, and yet there is no doubt that He said them.

Many things were said and done by Christ which are not recorded by any of the Evangelists, but by the fresh memory of those who were present.

Such things were delivered afterwards, as it were, from hand to hand, from the very times of the Apostles, down to us. [37]

Luther does not doubt that Christ said in His Last Supper, *'as often as ye shall do this'*, ye shall do it in commemoration of Me.

---

[36] At the Last Supper with his apostles on the eve of his passion Jesus anticipated, that is, both symbolized his free self-offering and made it really present: *"This is my Body which is given for you"* (Luke 22:19), *"This is my Blood which is poured out..."* (Matthew 26:28) Thus he both instituted the Eucharist as the *"memorial"* (1 Corinthians 11:25) of his sacrifice and instituted his apostles as priests of the new Covenant (*Compendium*, Number 120).

[37] Apostolic Tradition occurs in two ways: through the living transmission of the word of God (also simply called Tradition) and through Sacred Scripture which is the same proclamation of salvation in written form (*Compendium*, Number 13).

He is so sure that they were Christ's words that from them he takes his argument: *'nobody is obliged to receive the Sacrament; it is left to every man's discretion, and we are only bound, as often as we do it, to do it in remembrance of Christ.'*

These very words he does not read in the Evangelists concerning the Supper of Our Lord: for nothing else is read there, but, *'do this in commemoration of me.'*

Where, then, does Luther read these words, *'as often as ye shall do these things'?* Where else, if not in the Mass?

Indeed, I believe nowhere else for the Apostles did not use these words.

Luther trusts so much in these words and uses them, because he finds them in the Canon of the Mass.

Why then doesn't he give the same credit to that part of the same Canon in which the Mass is called offering and sacrifice?

Luther admits only Scripture. Yet, he confesses that the priests do rightly receive what they consecrate in Mass, even though neither in Scripture nor anywhere else it is clearly testified that Christ did it in His Last Supper.

He should not wonder if the priest offers Christ to His Father as Christ Himself did on the Cross, as it is witnessed by clear Scripture in several places.

Luther's own arguments demonstrate that the Cross belongs to the Testament made at the Supper, when he says that *'the Testament involves the death of the Testator, by which alone it can be made perfect.'*

Moreover, it seems, as it is said, that the mingling of water with the wine had its beginning from no other place; now the death of the Testator is not said by Scripture to be done at the Last Supper, but on the Cross.

Let Luther, therefore, refrain from presenting his trifling argument that *'because Christ did not offer Himself at His Last Supper, therefore the priest must not be believed to offer Him in Mass.'*

Now in the Mass the celebrant does not only represent what Christ performed in His Last Supper, but also what He did on the Cross, where He consummated what He began in the Supper.

Now we come to the last of Luther's arguments, whereby he uses it like a sacred anchor to sustain his ship.

This argument is the most frivolous of all the rest:

'How can it be, (says he) *that the priest should offer to God what he takes himself? It is not likely that the Mass should be a Sacrifice, when we receive it ourselves. The same thing cannot be received and offered at*

one and the same time, nor given and received by one and the same person.'

Luther discourages us everywhere from philosophical reasoning, and yet, in so sacred a thing, he endeavours to sustain his argument by the merest sophistry in the world.

Was there ever a sacrifice in Moses' Law which was not taken by those who offered it? Did God Himself eat what they offered Him? *'Shall I eat the flesh of bullocks? Or shall I drink the blood of goats?'* says the Lord' (Ps 49:13)?

Besides, since Christ was both Priest and Sacrifice, why couldn't He establish that the priest, who supplies the same sacrifice, might both offer and receive the Victim himself?

But lest in this case I may seem to imitate Luther, who has nothing to say for himself except what issues out of his own idle brain, I will lay before you what St. Ambrose says about the Mass:

'O Lord God, (he says) *with how great contrition of heart, with what fountains of tears, with how great reverence and fear, with what chastity and purity of mind that divine and celestial mystery is to be celebrated. Where Thy Flesh is truly received; where Thy Blood is truly drank; where the lowest is joined to the highest and divine things with human; where the Saints and Angels are present; where, after an admirable and unspeakable manner, Thyself art both Priest and Sacrifice! Who shall be able to celebrate this Mystery worthily, if Almighty God does not render him worthy?'*

Here you see how the saintly Father calls the Mass an oblation, and says that Christ Himself is both Priest and Sacrifice in it, even as He was on the Cross.

Let Luther see how much authority he attributes to Saint Ambrose.

St. Gregory makes clear how much esteem he had for Ambrose, when he imitated him in his writings:

'Which of the faithful (he says) *can doubt that in the very time of the immolation, the heavens are opened to the words of the priest, in that Mystery of Christ? That Choirs of Angels are present; that the lowest things are associated to the highest; that earth is joined with heaven; and that of visible and invisible is made one thing?'*

And in another place: *'for this singular Victim, which renews to us the Death of the Only-Begotten, does loose our souls from eternal Death.'*

Nor does he speak less to the purpose, when he says, *'hence therefore let us ponder with ourselves, how much that sacrifice stands us in stead, which always imitates the Passion of the Only-Begotten Son.'*

We see that not only St. Ambrose but also St. Gregory calls the Mass an Immolation and Sacrifice.

They confess that not only the Last Supper of Christ is represented in it (as Luther holds), but also His Passion.

These Fathers were not alone of that judgment, because St. Augustine confesses the same thing in various places, speaking of the Mass in these terms:

'The Oblation is every day renewed, though Christ has but once suffered: because we daily fall, Christ is daily offered for us.

'Also, the Eucharist is a blessed offering by which we are blessed; an enrolment, by which we all are enrolled in heaven; a ratification, whereby we are mustered in the Heart of Christ.'

We have seen, therefore, that men so holy and learned have called the Mass an offering and a sacrifice, and they are of the belief that not only the Last Supper of Christ, but also His Passion, is commemorated by it.

They confess that immense and great advantages proceed from it, and the Church, agreeing with them, sings the same in the whole Mass. [38]

Therefore, I am much amazed at the way in which Luther dares to cry out that, on the contrary, the Mass is no sacrifice or offering, and that it brings no profit to the people.

By his most vain device he derides the authority of so many holy Fathers - or rather of the whole Church - as if they were all to be understood as relics of the Jewish ceremonies, in which he says, *'the Priest did heave up what was offered by the people'*.

This comment of Luther's seems so foolish and absurd, even to himself, that he had misgivings as to whether he should withstand the sentiments of the holy Fathers and the customs of the whole Church with such a babbling argument, or rather openly despise them:

'What, (he says), shall we say to the canons and authorities of the Fathers? I answer, (says he), that if we have nothing at all to say against them it is safer to deny all things than to confess that Mass is a work or sacrifice, lest we deny the words of Christ, corrupting them together with the Mass.

'Nevertheless, that we may agree with them also, we will say that all these things were the Relics of Jewish ceremonies.'

---

[38] Holy Communion increases our union with Christ and with his Church. It preserves and renews the life of grace received at Baptism and Confirmation and makes us grow in love for our neighbour. It strengthens us in charity, wipes away venial sins and preserves us from mortal sin in the future (*Compendium*, Number 292).

Therefore, if nothing more is to be said about it, the holy Fathers and the whole Church might be thought to speak foolishly.

Thus Luther, this *civil man*, tendering the repute of the Fathers and the honour of the Church, seems to oblige them by covering their shame with the veil of *his most excellent devices*: he refers to them as the *'Relics of the Jewish rites.'*

If anybody removes it, it will be to his danger.

Should anyone press him more narrowly, Luther does not have the perspicacity to realise that he would rather blow away all the testimonies of the holy Fathers and the customs of the Church than admit that the Mass is a good work or a sacrifice.

That is, rather than allow what is true to be true: *'for in that* (says he) *they deny Christ's Words, and corrupt Faith with Mass,* [they] *who affirm Mass to be a sacrifice.'*

I suppose that no one will believe him, unless...

He first shows that he has read another Gospel different from that which the holy Fathers ever read; or

That in reading the same he has been more diligent than they were; or

He has understood it better; or finally that

He is more careful about the Faith than any man ever was before him.

But I believe he will not offer any other Gospel to us. If he does, it will not be accepted though an Angel from Heaven should descend with it.

And the Gospel that he offers has not been more diligently examined nor more narrowly pried into by him than it has been tried and searched into by others to this day.

For nobody has ever said that they found in the Gospel what Luther boasts himself to have found, that is, *'the Mass is not a good Work; it is not an Oblation, nor a Sacrifice.'*

If anyone diligently considers what has been written by the Fathers and by Luther, he cannot be ignorant of the difference made in their care about Faith: those holy, ancient Fathers have observed that this is the principal of all Sacraments, containing as it does the Lord of Sacraments.[39]

---

[39] The sacraments not only presuppose faith but with words and ritual elements they nourish, strengthen, and express it. By celebrating the sacraments, the Church professes the faith that comes from the apostles. This explains the origin of the ancient saying, *"lex orandi, lex credendi,"* that is, the Church believes as she prays (*Compendium*, Number 228).

Thus, it is the only Sacrifice which alone remains, instead of so many sacrifices of the Old Law.

And lastly, of all the works that can be done for the salvation of the people, this one, without comparison, is the best and most wholesome.

Other Sacraments are only profitable to the particular persons receiving them; this one, in the Mass, is beneficial to all, in general.

When one man prays to God for another, his prayers may not only be hindered but also made ineffectual through his fault.

But in His merciful goodness, God instituted the Mass for the salvation of the faithful.

In the Mass, His own Body is offered as such a wholesome sacrifice that the wickedness of the minister, be it ever so great, is not able to lessen or avert its benefit to people.

Seeing these things, the most holy Fathers took all possible care and used their utmost endeavours so that the greatest Faith imaginable should be had towards this most propitiatory Sacrament, and it should be worshipped with the greatest honour possible. [40]

And, for that reason, amongst many other things, they also delivered us this teaching with great care: *'the Bread and Wine do not remain in the Eucharist, but are truly changed into the Body and Blood of Christ'*.

They taught the Mass to be a Sacrifice, in which Christ Himself is truly offered for the sins of the Christian people.

So far as it was lawful for mortals, they adorned this immortal Mystery with venerable worship and mystical rites.

They commanded the people to be present in adoration of it while it is celebrated, so as to procure their salvation. [41]

---

[40] The worship due to the sacrament of the Eucharist, whether during the celebration of the Mass or outside it, is the worship of latria, that is, the adoration given to God alone. The Church guards with the greatest care Hosts that have been consecrated. She brings them to the sick and to other persons who find it impossible to participate at Mass. She also presents them for the solemn adoration of the faithful and she bears them in processions. The Church encourages the faithful to make frequent visits to adore the Blessed Sacrament reserved in the tabernacle (*Compendium*, Number 286).

[41] In the Eucharist the sacrifice of Christ becomes also the sacrifice of the members of his Body. The lives of the faithful, their praise, their suffering, their prayers, their work, are united to those of Christ. In as much as it is a sacrifice, the Eucharist is likewise offered for all the faithful, living and dead, in reparation for the sins of all and to obtain spiritual and temporal benefits from God. The

Finally, lest the laity, by refraining from receiving the Sacrament, should little by little omit it completely, the Fathers have established an obligation that every man must receive at least once a year.

It is by those things and many of like nature in several ages, that the holy Fathers of the Church have demonstrated their care for the Faith and veneration of this adorable Sacrament.

Therefore, Luther should not assert (even though he does) that those who call the Mass a 'Sacrifice' - or say that it is profitable to no one except to him who receives the Sacrament in it - corrupt the Word of Christ, the Faith and the Mass itself.

It will not be amiss to consider here in what manner Luther sustains upon his shoulders the word of Christ, Faith, and Mass itself, so that they may not become corrupted or fall.

First of all, he changes the name of the Sacrament itself into a worse name.

What was called the Eucharist for so many ages, or the Sacrament of Christ's Body, Luther commands to be called *'bread'*, lest its name should bring its majesty to the hearer's mind.

Afterwards, Luther taught that the bread and wine, which the Ancients held to be turned into the Body and Blood of our Lord, do remain wholly bread and wine.

In this manner, little by little, he may redirect the honour from Christ to the bread.

After this, although Luther does not condemn the Church for having adorned and amplified the Mass with rites and ceremonies, he thinks that it would be more Christian-like if the pomp of vestments, singing, gestures and other ceremonies were laid aside.

Thus, the Mass might be more like and near to the first Mass of all, which Christ celebrated in His Last Supper with His Apostles.

Or, rather, that nothing may be left that might move the simple minds of the common people, and bring them to the worship of this invisible Deity, through the majesty of visible honour.

Moreover, he teaches, and, as much as he is able to, inculcates that the Mass is not a good work, not a sacrifice, not an oblation, nor profitable to any of the people.

To what purpose, pray, is this so *evangelical* a lecture?

Church in heaven is also united to the offering of Christ (*Compendium*, Number 281.)

It is so that all the people - being persuaded that the Mass is profitable only to the priest - may leave the Mass to him and neglect it themselves, thereby paying no duty to something deemed unprofitable to them.

Lastly, so that, when they receive Communion, if they have nothing but Faith, they may know that they are about to receive the Testament - regardless the state of their conscience.

The more erroneous they are, and the more troubled with the sting and concupiscence of sin they may be, the more they are to assure themselves that they are partakers of the divine promises, because this Sacrament is the medicine of sins past, present, and to come.

The Sacrament would find no room for itself in those who, with greatest anxiety, purge themselves from the diseases of sin and, according to the precept of the Apostle (I Cor.11:28), proving themselves, they may approach our Lord's Table with as pure and sincere a conscience as may be possible.

Thus, since they cannot say we are justified, at least they may say that we are guilty of nothing to ourselves.

Luther has taught this short and compendious preparation for receiving the Eucharist, that is, *'in the faith alone of the promise, without any good works, and a light examination of conscience.'*

Afterwards, so that nothing may be absent from the absolute sanctity of receiving the Sacrament, he shows his desire concerning what time, and how often he believes the people should receive; and that is, at no time at all.

And why should that be so?

Is there anyone so blind as to not see the end result of Luther's argument?

Certainly, for no other reason than the people may, by degrees, cease to receive Communion altogether.

At first, Luther changed the daily Communion into a seventh-day communicating. Then, afterwards, he changed it to a longer time. Lastly, he desired that Communion could be forsaken altogether.

As if fearing that this should happen, the Fathers decreed that every man should receive Holy Communion three times a year, threatening that he who disobeys should not be accounted a Christian.

Nevertheless, they could not continue that custom for long.

So, at last, the matter fell so low that it could descend no lower: now we are obliged to receive only once a year. [42]

Now if Luther could demolish this custom, as he endeavours, the world would in time be reduced - through the decay of the fervour of Faith - to what it should have come to long ago, if it had not been prevented by this solemn custom of receiving at least once a year.

Ultimately, there would scarcely remain the least hint of Communion among the people and perhaps the clergy as well.

This would happen if Luther could spoil the Mass not only of its preparation and ceremonies but also of the people's hope and veneration of, and resort to it.

These are the excellent promises of Luther.

This is that spacious liberty he promises to all those who forsake the Catholic Church to follow him: that they may be freed at last from the use and Faith of the Sacrament!

I refrain therefore from speaking on this subject any more, which is so clear in itself that it needs no further dispute.

Since we have discovered the crafty windings of the subtle serpent, as undoubtedly they are seen by all who are not quite blind, it is unnecessary to exhort anybody to shun such apparent evils.

I believe that none are so mad, as to forsake the Church of God for the Synagogue of Satan.

To serve Christ is to reign.

Thus, to shun His service and to enlist oneself into the *liberty* proposed by Luther is to put one's foot into the snare of the devil, knowingly and willingly, under the name of *liberty*.

Rather, let all the Faithful of Christ say with the Psalmist, *'we will not decline from Thy judgments, because Thou hast appointed us a Law'* (Ps. 118:102).

---

[42] The Church recommends that the faithful, if they have the required dispositions, receive Holy Communion whenever they participate at Holy Mass. However, the Church obliges them to receive Holy Communion at least once a year during the Easter season (*Compendium*, Number 290).

Chapter V

Of Baptism

 OR THE REST of the Sacraments, it is not necessary to dwell upon them. Luther takes most of them away from us.
He has handled the Sacrament of the Eucharist - almost the only one he vouchsafed to leave us - in such a manner that no one can doubt he devised to demolish Baptism also, little by little.

This we have already shown you. [43]

He does not praise any of the Sacraments, unless to the prejudice of another. He extols Baptism so much that he devalues Penance.

He has treated Baptism itself in such a manner that it would have been better had he not touched it at all.

First of all, in order that he may *appear* to treat a matter so holy with a great deal of sanctity, he, by a long discourse, teaches that the divine promise is to be believed, whereby he promises salvation to them that believe, and are baptised.

He angrily reproaches the Church for not teaching this Faith to Christians, as if they were so ignorant of the Christian Faith as not to understand this.

Luther proposes it as a new thing, almost unheard of, to the reproach of all the Church Doctors.

But this is no new method of his; to trifle in things known as though they had never before been heard of.

Having in many words shown what this *'faith'* is, he afterwards extols the riches of faith in order that he may render us poor of good works, without which, as St. James says, *'so faith also, if it have not works, is dead in itself'* (2:17-26).

But Luther commends Faith to us not only to permit us to abstain from good works, but also *to encourage us to commit any kind of action, however bad it may be.*

'You see now (he says) *how rich the baptised man is, he who cannot lose his salvation - though willing to lose it - by any sin whatever, except infidelity: For no sins can damn him, only incredulity.'*

O most impious doctrine and mistress of all impiety!

It is in itself so hateful to pious ears that there is no need to confute it.

Adultery will not damn then! Murder will not damn! Perjury will not damn! Isn't parricide damnable either, if every one believes that he shall be saved through the virtue of the promise alone in Baptism?

This he openly asserts.

---

[43] This sacrament is primarily called Baptism because of the central rite with which it is celebrated. To baptize means to "immerse" in water. The one who is baptized is immersed into the death of Christ and rises with him as a *"new creature"* (2 Corinthians 5:17). This sacrament is also called the *"bath of regeneration and renewal in the Holy Spirit"* (Titus 3:5); and it is called *"enlightenment"* because the baptized becomes "a son of light" (Ephesians 5:8) – (*Compendium*, Number 252).

The words he presently adds do not correct this sentence in any manner, but rather add to its force:

'If faith return or stand in the divine promise made by the baptised, all other things are swallowed in a moment in the same faith by the truth of God, if you confess Him, and stick faithfully to His promise, for He cannot deny Himself.'

What else does Luther say by these words except what he has said before, that, *'infidelity excepted, all other crimes are in a moment swallowed up by Faith alone; if you confess Christ, and stick faithfully to His Promise.'*

That is, if you firmly believe that you are to be saved by Faith, you are, notwithstanding whatever you do. [44]

And, that you may doubt even less what he aims at; *'contrition* (he says), *confession of sins, satisfaction and all these human inventions will forsake you. They will leave you unhappier if you busy yourselves with them and forget this divine Truth.'*

What *'Truth'*, pray?

'This one: that no sins can damn you, save infidelity alone.'

Which Christian ears can patiently hear the pestilentious hissing of this serpent, whereby he extols Baptism for no other end, but to devalue Penance, and establish the grace of Baptism for a free liberty to sin? [45]

Contrary to this doctrine is that sentence of St. Jerome that says, *'Penance is the table after shipwreck.'*

But this does not agree with Luther.

He denies and disputes sin to be the shipwreck of Faith, as if that single word - *sin* - should totally destroy all the strength of Faith.

---

[44] To the young man who asked this question, Jesus answered, *"If you would enter into life, keep the commandments"*, and then he added, *"Come, follow Me"* (Matthew 19:16-21). To follow Jesus involves keeping the commandments. The law has not been abolished but man is invited to rediscover it in the Person of the divine Master who realized it perfectly in himself, revealed its full meaning and attested to its permanent validity (*Compendium*, Number 434).

[45] There are some acts which, in and of themselves, are always illicit by reason of their object (for example, blasphemy, homicide, adultery). Choosing such acts entails a disorder of the will, that is, a moral evil which can never be justified by appealing to the good effects which could possibly result from them (*Compendium*, Number 369).

Who, besides Luther, is ignorant that a sinner is not only *not save*d by the Faith of Baptism alone, but also that the Baptism will add to his damnation?

And indeed deservedly, because he has offended God, from Whom he had the whole grace of Baptism, and God demands more from him to whom He has given more.

Therefore, since Faith becomes dead by wicked works, why can't we also say that he who falls from the grace of God into the hands of the devil suffers shipwreck?

And, without Penance, he cannot escape the shipwreck or be renewed to a condition whereby Baptism may be profitable to him.

Has St. Jerome written wickedly in this?

Does the whole Church follow an impious belief for not believing Luther - who says that Christians are safe enough by Faith alone, without Penance, in the midst of their sins?

Moreover, he is so consumed by the *Faith of the Sacrament* that he does not care much for the form of words; though the word, by which the water is signified, ought to be of no less moment than the water itself.

If he thinks that any care is to be taken regarding it, it is that it may be pure and elementary.

Likewise, shouldn't some true form also be carefully instituted, and used, as is approved and now observed in the Church, and was formerly in use amongst the Ancients?

After this, Luther magnifies *faith* so much that he almost seems to insinuate that Faith alone is sufficient, without the Sacrament.

In the meanwhile, he deprives the Sacrament of grace.

When he says *'the Sacrament itself profits nothing,'* he denies that the Sacraments confer any grace or are effectual signs of grace, or that the Sacraments of the Gospel Law differ in any kind from those of the Mosaic Law - as far as the efficacy of grace is concerned. [46]

I shall not dispute much about this matter. However, it seems to me that as all things were but figures with the Jews - whose Truth we have in the Christian Law - it may not be absurd to believe that the Sacraments

---

[46] The sacraments are efficacious *ex opere operato* ("by the very fact that the sacramental action is performed") because it is Christ who acts in the sacraments and communicates the grace they signify. The efficacy of the sacraments does not depend upon the personal holiness of the minister. However, the fruits of the sacraments do depend on the dispositions of the one who receives them (*Compendium*, Number 229).

which the Church uses far excel those of the Synagogues, just as the New Law surpasses the Old Law. [47]

In other words: *the Body is greater than the shadow.* [48]

I am neither the first nor the only one to hold this view.

Hugo de Saint-Victor, whom none esteems other than as a good and learned man, has spoken thus:

'We say that all Sacraments are certain signs, whereby spiritual graces are conferred.

'Moreover, the signs of spiritual graces, according to the process of time, ought to be framed more evidently and plainly, so that the knowledge of Truth might increase with the effect of salvation.'

And a little further, *'because circumcision could only lop off exterior enormities but not cleanse the inward filth of pollutions, a washing font of water succeeded circumcision, which purges the whole, that perfect justice may be signified.'*

I hope nobody will deny that this Doctor believes that the Sacrament of Baptism cleanses internally and signifies perfect justice more efficaciously than circumcision ever did.

In this regard, Luther takes notice of two views and opposes both of them:

The first one is of those *'who have supposed some secret and hidden virtue to be in the word and water, which should work the grace of God in the soul of the baptised;'*

The other one is or those *'who attribute no virtue to the Sacraments, but were of opinion that grace was conferred by God alone, Who, according to His Covenant, is present in the Sacraments He instituted.'*

---

[47] In the Old Covenant Baptism was pre-figured in various ways: water, seen as source of life and of death; in the Ark of Noah, which saved by means of water; in the passing through the Red Sea, which liberated Israel from Egyptian slavery; in the crossing of the Jordan River, that brought Israel into the promised land which is the image of eternal life (*Compendium*, Number 253).

[48] All the Old Covenant prefigurations find their fulfilment in Jesus Christ. At the beginning of his public life Jesus had himself baptized by John the Baptist in the Jordan. On the cross, blood and water, signs of Baptism and the Eucharist, flowed from his pierced side. After his Resurrection he gave to his apostles this mission*: "Go forth and make disciples of all nations, baptizing them in the name of the Father and of the Son and of the Holy Spirit"* (Matthew 28:19) – (*Compendium*, Number 254).

But because all agree that Sacraments are efficacious signs of grace, Luther rejects the one as well as the other. [49]

For my part, I do not know which of the views is the truest, so neither dare I be so bold as to contemn either of them.

That very belief which now is the less assented to, namely, *'the water, by virtue of the word, has a hidden power of purging the soul,'* does not seem to be altogether absurd.

If we believe that fire has any influence over the soul, either to punish or purge sins, what prevents that water should penetrate to wash away the uncleanness of the soul, by the power of God by Whom also the other thing is done? [50]

This belief seems to be much confirmed by the words of St. Augustine when he says, *'the water of Baptism touches the body, and washes the heart.'*

And also that of St. Bede who says, *'Christ, by the touch of His most pure Flesh, has given the water a regenerating power.'*

Likewise that of the Prophet Ezechiel seems to tend towards this, *'I washed thee with water, and cleansed thy blood from thee'* (Ezech. 16:9).

Such words were spoken in times past, before Baptism was instituted. Notwithstanding this, they are understood according to the custom of the Prophets to be of the future.

Ezechiel does not speak only of the washing of the body, something unworthy of the preaching of a Prophet.

Rather, he speaks of the only washing which washes the crimes of the soul, that is, the Sacrament of Baptism.

Ezechiel seems to have spoken of Baptism in the person of God, prophesying that there should be a future cleansing by the washing font of water in the Sacrament of Baptism.

---

[49] That grace is the gratuitous gift that God gives us to make us participants in his Trinitarian life and able to act by his love. It is called habitual, sanctifying or deifying grace because it sanctifies and divinizes us. It is supernatural because it depends entirely on God's gratuitous initiative and surpasses the abilities of the intellect and the powers of human beings. It therefore escapes our experience (*Compendium*, Number 423).

[50] The essential rite of this sacrament consists in immersing the candidate in water or pouring water over his or her head while invoking the name of the Father and the Son and the Holy Spirit (*Compendium*, Number 256).

This Sacrament is made plainer by the same Prophet a little after when he speaks of the future: *'I will pour out'*, he says, *'clear water upon you, and I will cleanse you from all your iniquities'* (Ezech. 36:25).

Does he not promise here a cleansing by water?

Zacharias seems to unfold the matter more clearly, when he says, *'living water shall go out from Jerusalem; half of them to the East Sea, and half of them to the last Sea'* (Zach 14:8).

Does not this discourse manifest to us the figure of Baptism, that is, water flowing from the Church, which should purge both original and actual sin?

And he does not call it dead, but living, so that he might demonstrate - as I believe - that by the secret sanctification of God, the force of spiritual life is infused into a corporeal element.

As I have said already, neither do I presume to judge, nor am I curious after what manner God infuses grace by the Sacraments, because His ways are inscrutable (Rom 11:33).

Yet I believe that, in one way or another, this water should not be idle, since He foretells that so many and great things were to be done by water.

Unless all those things were spoken in vain, water, salt and other corporeal things do receive spiritual force by the word of God, without the Sacrament of Faith.

Thus, lights, fire, water, salt, bread, the altar, vestments, rings are either adjured by exorcisms or blessed by the invocation of grace. [51]

I say that if those things receive any virtue or presence of the Divinity without the Sacrament, how much more credible is it that the water flowing from Christ's side infuses a spiritual power of life into the fountain of regeneration?

Christ Himself speaks of this when He says that *'unless a man be born again of water and the Holy Ghost, he cannot enter into the kingdom of God'* (John 3:5), *'to which we are called in Baptism,'* as the Apostle says (1 Cor. 1).

---

[51] Sacramental signs come from created things (light, water, fire, bread, wine, oil); others come from social life (washing, anointing, breaking of bread). Still others come from the history of salvation in the Old Covenant (the Passover rites, the sacrifices, the laying on of hands, the consecrations). These signs, some of which are normative and unchangeable, were taken up by Christ and are made the bearers of his saving and sanctifying action (*Compendium*, Number 237).

Regarding Baptism, I am not against Luther for having attributed so much to Faith.

But, on the other hand, I oppose his attributing so much to Faith as though by it an evil life could be defended or the Sacraments exterminated.

But when he requires a certain and unquestionable Faith in the receiver of the Sacraments, for my part, I think it is to be wished for, rather than exacted.

When St. Peter exhorted the people after this manner, *'do penance: and be baptised every one of you in the name of Jesus Christ, for the remission of your sins. And you shall receive the gift of the Holy Ghost.'* (Acts 2:38), I do not doubt that he was ready to receive all the people to Baptism. [52]

Yet, he would not have exacted from them immediately that high, certain and indubitable *Faith* of Luther, which no one could have known to have attained.

But he did promise remission of sins and grace from the Sacrament itself to all those who would simply present themselves and desire it. [53]

An undoubted and certain Faith is a very great thing, but it happens neither always nor to everybody. Not even to them who do not doubt that they have it.

I indeed shall not doubt to hope that the benignity of God assists in His Sacraments, and infuses invisible grace by means of visible signs.

Thus, by the fervour of His Sacraments, He helps the tepidity of believers so that many may obtain salvation by the Sacraments, those who can promise no more to themselves of their Faith than he could, who said, *'I do believe, Lord. Help my unbelief'* (Mk 9:23).

Regarding this, if anyone - besides my adversary - thinks I attribute too much to the Sacrament, let him know that I define nothing and I

---

[52] From the day of Pentecost, the Church has administered Baptism to anyone who believes in Jesus Christ (*Compendium*, Number 255).

[53] Baptism takes away original sin, all personal sins and all punishment due to sin. It makes the baptized person a participant in the divine life of the Trinity through sanctifying grace, the grace of justification which incorporates one into Christ and into his Church. It gives one a share in the priesthood of Christ and provides the basis for communion with all Christians. It bestows the theological virtues and the gifts of the Holy Spirit. A baptized person belongs forever to Christ. He is marked with the indelible seal of Christ (character) – (*Compendium*, Number 263).

appoint nothing in any way which may be harmful to Faith, from which I derogate nothing.

But just as I do not think that Faith alone, without the Sacrament, is sufficient for him who may receive it, so neither can the Sacrament suffice him without Faith, but that both ought to concur and cooperate with their power. [54]

I think it safer to allow something to the Sacrament rather than, like Luther, to attribute so much to Faith as to leave neither grace nor the efficacy of a sign to the Sacrament.

Besides, he makes Faith nothing else but a cloak for a wicked life, as we have previously shown.

And that this may appear more clearly, after he has deprived the Sacraments of grace, he robs the Church of all vows and laws.

He is not moved at all that God said, *'vow ye, and pay to the Lord your God'* (Ps 75:12), and *'if thou hast vowed anything to God, defer not to pay it: for an unfaithful and foolish promise displeaseth Him: but whatsoever thou hast vowed, pay it.'* (Eccles 5:3).

Regarding vows, I do not doubt that some of those whom he calls 'vovists' and 'votaries,' will answer for their own profession, because Luther turns them, at once and almost all together, out of the Church.

---

[54] Everyone who is to be baptized is required to make a profession of faith. This is done personally in the case of an adult or by the parents and by the Church in the case of infants. Also the godfather or the godmother and the whole ecclesial community share the responsibility for baptismal preparation (catechumenate) as well as for the development and safeguarding of the faith and grace given at baptism (*Compendium*, Number 259).

The Laws of Rulers are to be obeyed

 OR THE LAWS, I am amazed that Luther could shamelessly invent such ridiculous things; as if Christians could not sin and as if so great a multitude of believers should be so perfect that nothing needs to be ordered, either for the honour of God, or the avoidance of wickedness.

By the same work and policy, he robs princes and prelates of all power and authority.

For what shall a king or a prelate do, if he cannot appoint any law or execute the law that was appointed before, even like a ship without a rudder, suffering his people to float without ever coming to port?

Where, then, is that saying of the Apostle, *'let every soul be subject to higher powers'* (Rom' 13:1). [55]

Where is that other word of his, *'for he is God's minister to thee, for good. But if thou do that which is evil, fear: for he beareth not the sword in vain. For he is God's minister: an avenger to execute wrath upon him that doth evil.'* (Rom' 13:4)?

Where is also that other one, *'obey your prelates and be subject to them. For they watch as being to render an account of your souls'* (Heb 13:17)? [56]

And what follows?

Why, then, does St. Paul say, *'the Law is good?'* (1 Tim 1:8; Prov. 13:14) and in another place, *'but above all these things have charity, which is the bond of perfection'* (Col. 3:14)?

Furthermore, why does St. Augustine say, *'the power of the king, the right of the owner, the instruments of the executioner, the arms of the soldier, the discipline of the governor, and the severity of a good father were not instituted in vain?'*

They first have all their customs, causes, reasons, and profits; when the others are feared, evil men are restrained from doing evil and the good live quietly among the wicked.

But I refrain to speak of Kings, lest I should seem to plead my own case.

I only ask this: if no one, neither man nor Angel, can appoint any law among Christians, why does the Apostle institute for us so many laws,

---

[55] Christ instituted an ecclesiastical hierarchy with the mission of feeding the people of God in his name and for this purpose gave it authority. The hierarchy is formed of sacred ministers, bishops, priests, and deacons. Thanks to the sacrament of Orders, bishops and priests act in the exercise of their ministry in the name and person of Christ the Head. Deacons minister to the people of God in the diakonia (service) of word, liturgy, and charity (*Compendium*, Number 179).

[56] Jesus chose the twelve, the future witnesses of his Resurrection, and made them sharers of his mission and of his authority to teach, to absolve from sins, and to build up and govern the Church. In this college, Peter received *"the keys of the Kingdom"* (Matthew 16:19) and assumed the first place with the mission to keep the faith in its integrity and to strengthen his brothers (*Compendium*, Number 109).

such as for electing bishops (1 Tim 3; Tit 1:7), for widows (1 Tim 3 ff), covering the heads of women (1 Cor. 11:5 ff)?

Why has he ordained that a Christian woman should not forsake her husband, though an infidel, if she is not abandoned by him first (1 Cor. 7:12-13)?

Why dare he say, *'for to the rest I speak, not the Lord'* (1 Cor. 7:12)?

Why has he exercised so great power, as to command the incestuous man to be delivered over to Satan, to the destruction of the flesh (1 Cor. 5:4-5)?

Why has St. Peter struck Ananias and Sapphira his wife (Acts 5) with the like punishment, for reserving to themselves a little of their own money?

If the Apostles,[57] both of themselves and by the especial command of Our Lord, appoint so many things to be observed by Christians, why may not those who succeed them, do the same for the good of the people?

St. Ambrose, Bishop of Milan - a holy man, not arrogant - has scrupled in commanding that married persons in his diocese should abstain from their lawful rights during the whole time of Lent.

Is Luther so shocked that the Pope of Rome - Successor of St. Peter, Christ's Vicar - should institute a fast or prayers?

It is believed by all Christians that Christ gave the keys of the Church to him, as the Prince of the Apostles, and by him the rest should enter, or be kept out.[58]

As for his persuading men to obey outwardly in body and yet retain to themselves their liberty in mind, who is so blind as not to see Luther's shifts and quirks?

Why does this simple man, this hypocrite, carry both water and fire?

Why does he - as it were in the words of the Apostle - command all not to serve men, not to be subject to the statutes of men (1 Cor. 7:23)

---

[57] The Church is apostolic in her origin because she has been built on *"the foundation of the Apostles"* (Ephesians 2:20). She is apostolic in her teaching which is the same as that of the Apostles. She is apostolic by reason of her structure insofar as she is taught, sanctified, and guided until Christ returns by the Apostles through their successors who are the bishops in communion with the successor of Peter (*Compendium*, Number 174).

[58] The College of bishops in union with the Pope, and never without him, also exercises supreme and full authority over the Church (*Compendium*, Number 183).

and yet, notwithstanding this, command to show obedience to the *'unjust tyranny of the Pope'*?

Did the Apostle preach after this manner? *'Kings have no right over you, yet suffer you an unjust empire. Masters have no right of power over you, yet suffer an unjust servitude'.*

If Luther is of the opinion that people ought not to obey, why does he also say they must obey?

If he thinks they ought to obey, why is he not himself obedient?

Why does this quack juggle so?

Why does he thus reproachfully raise himself against the Bishop of Rome, whom he says we ought to obey?

Why does he raise this tumult?

Why does he excite the people against the Pope, whose tyranny, as he calls it, is to be endured?

Indeed, I believe that it is for no other end than to procure for himself the good esteem of such malefactors as those who desire to escape the punishment due to their crimes.

In this way, he hopes they might choose him for their head, since he now fights for their liberty and demolishes the Church of Christ, founded so long ago upon a firm Rock.

Thus, they erect to themselves a new Church, compacted of vicious and impious persons, contrary to that exclamation of the prophet:

'I have hated the assembly of the malignant; and with the wicked I will not sit' (Ps 25:5). *'Direct me in Thy truth, and teach me; for Thou art God my Saviour; and on Thee have I waited all the day long'* (Ps 24:5).

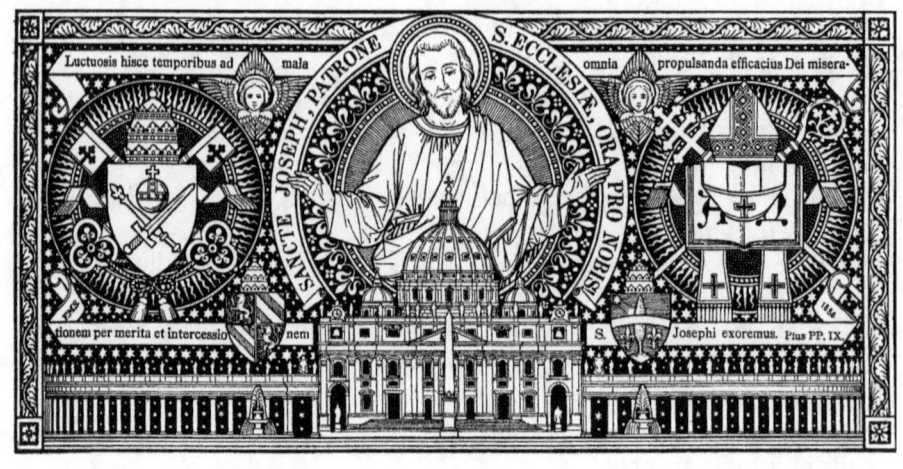

Chapter VI

Of the Sacrament of Penance

AM GREATLY TROUBLED to hear how absurd, impious and contradictory are the trifles and babbles, wherewith Luther bespatters the sacrament of Penance. [59]

---

[59] This sacrament is called the sacrament of Penance, the sacrament of Reconciliation, the sacrament of Forgiveness, the sacrament of Confession, and the sacrament of Conversion (*Compendium*, Number 296).

First, after his old custom, he proposes a new thing which is commonly known by everybody, that is, *'we ought to believe the promise of God, whereby He promises remission of sins to those who repent.'*

Then, he reproachfully cries out against the Church for not teaching this Faith.

Who, I pray you, exhorts anyone to the penance of Judas, that is, to be sorry for what he has committed and not expect pardon?

Who would say that we ought to pray for remission of sins, if he did not also teach pardon to be promised to the penitent?

What is more frequently preached than the clemency of Almighty God, which is so great, that He mercifully extends it to all persons who are willing to reform their wicked lives? [60]

Did anyone, besides Luther, ever read that, *'when the wicked turneth himself away from his wickedness, which he hath wrought, and doeth judgment, and justice: he shall save his soul alive'* (Ezech. 18:27)?

Has none ever read, that the adulteress was dismissed (John 8:3)?

That the Prophet was pardoned, who was not only guilty of adultery, but of murder also (2 Kgs 12)?

That Paradise was given to the thief on the Cross (Lk 23:43), and at that time too, when he could not cancel his committed crimes by any satisfaction?

Those who instruct the people are so far from not teaching them this hope of obtaining pardon - which Luther cries is past - that they rather seem to do it too much.

The people are so easily inclined to rely upon this confidence that there is a greater need of recalling them to the other side, whereby they may contemplate the severe and inflexible justice of God.

For there are ten to be found, who sin by overconfidence in that promise of mercy, for every one who despairs of obtaining pardon.

Let Luther, then, no longer propose this teaching as something new and strange to us, which everybody already knows.

Let him not complain any longer that this is out of use, when it is but more than usual.

---

[60] Since the new life of grace received in Baptism does not abolish the weakness of human nature nor the inclination to sin (that is, concupiscence), Christ instituted this sacrament for the conversion of the baptized who have been separated from him by sin (*Compendium*, Number 297).

Chapter VII

Of Contrition

AVING THUS BLOTTED OUT, the promise and faith (says Luther), *let us see what they have substituted in their place.'*
'They allotted three parts to penance: contrition, confession, and satisfaction.' And he handles the three of them in such a manner, that it appears well enough that none of them pleases him. [61]

---

[61] They are: a careful examination of conscience; contrition (or repentance), which is perfect when it is motivated by love of God and imperfect if it rests on

First of all, he is very angry at contrition; he calls it the anger of God, unbearable; because place is given to attrition, and God is believed to supply, by the Sacrament, what is lacking in man in the sorrow for his sins when it is less vehement.

Let us see how well he maintains what he says, and what he brings against himself.

He teaches that contrition is a great thing, not easily had. He commands all men to be certain that they have it; to believe undoubtedly that through the words of the promise all their sins are forgiven them; and that, after they are loosed by the word of man here on earth, they are absolved by God in heaven.

Here is where his own assertion will either fall back upon what he has already reprehended, or else will appear much more absurd.

For God has either promised to forgive sins through penance to those who...

Grieve as much for their sins as required by their nature and greatness; or to those who...

Grieve not so much; or, finally, to such who are not sorry at all.

If God has promised forgiveness only to those who are as contrite as the greatness of their crimes requires, then Luther himself cannot be assured beyond doubt that his sins are forgiven him, as he commands all others to be.

How will he be certain of obtaining the promise for himself, when he cannot know for sure that he is sufficiently contrite for his sins?

No mortal man has ever yet known how great contrition is required for mortal sin.

If God has promised pardon to those who are less contrite than the greatness of their sins requires, then He has promised it to those called *Attrites*, and by that Luther agrees with those he now finds fault with.

But if God has promised pardon to those who have no sorrow for their sins, then surely He has made a much greater promise to those that are attrite; that is, to those who are sorry to some degree.

---

other motives and which includes the determination not to sin again; confession, which consists in the telling of one's sins to the priest; and satisfaction or the carrying out of certain acts of penance which the confessor imposes upon the penitent to repair the damage caused by sin (*Compendium*, Number 303).

Wherefore, if he admits only contrition - that is, a sufficient grief - then nobody can be assured that he is absolved; and Luther's certain and undoubted confidence in absolution will perish, or be false and erroneous.

Luther reproves those who say that attrition becomes contrition by means of the Sacrament of Penance.

But he also says that the Sacrament of Penance does forgive the sins of those who - by confessing themselves sinners and asking and obtaining pardon by the mouth of their brother - perform only a slack or lukewarm penance.

How is this different from the view of those whom Luther reproves?

For what is wanting in men is supplied by the Sacrament. Otherwise, Luther's position, that *'man must be certain of absolution,'* is false.

Whether he wills it or not, he must at least admit the meaning of the word *attrition*, if not the word itself.

If he grants the meaning - as he will if he is not to fly from his own opinion - it is a very unseasonable trifle of his to contend concerning the word, and to allow the effect.

Again, he sets upon the whole Church with magnificent words, as though She taught contrition in a perverse manner, exhorting us to secure it by the collection and aspect of our sins.

We ought to have been taught in the first place - as he says - the beginnings and causes of contrition, namely, the immoveable truth of divine threats and promises.

He speaks as though such things were not taught everywhere among the people.

He alleges many passages of Scripture for that opinion, passages that are neither less threatening nor comfortable; likewise, the causes added together to procure contrition are not less efficacious than those Luther exacts, and are much more holy.

These causes propose almost nothing except the fear of punishment or the hopes of reward; which is a conversion not so acceptable to God as a conversion caused by love.

This may be done, not only by what Luther advises – that is, God's threats and promise of remission – but also by what they teach, which Luther derides.

He speaks as if the Church had taught nothing at all about the bounty of God towards us and His exceeding great benefits conferred upon us. God grants us good undeservingly, and demerits our evil from us. [62]

In this way, the sinner, having considered these things, will rather be touched with sorrow for having offended so pious a Father than so powerful a Lord; and he will dread his own punishment less than God's anger.

And he will not be as desirous of Heaven as of God's favour. [63]

This consideration of divine bounty forms contrition (*'knowest thou not, that the benignity of God leadeth thee to Penance'*? - Rom 2:4).

As I have said, this forms a holier contrition than that which is formed by Luther from the fear of punishment and hopes of pardon, he who boasts that nobody teaches threats but himself, whereas all men do teach them, and better too.

---

[62] In general merit refers to the right to recompense for a good deed. With regard to God, we of ourselves are not able to merit anything, having received everything freely from him. However, God gives us the possibility of acquiring merit through union with the love of Christ, who is the source of our merits before God. The merits for good works, therefore must be attributed in the first place to the grace of God and then to the free will of man (*Compendium*, Number 426).

[63] The essential elements [of the Sacrament of Penance] are two: the acts of the penitent who comes to repentance through the action of the Holy Spirit, and the absolution of the priest who in the name of Christ grants forgiveness and determines the ways of making satisfaction (*Compendium*, Number 302).

Chapter VIII

Of Confession

LUTHER TEACHES that *'in public crimes, where the sin is known to all people, Confession is to be made'*.
In the confession of secret sins, however, he is not so certain.
Although he does not seem to reject it altogether, yet one cannot tell whether he admits it as something commanded or not, because he denies that it can be proved by Scripture.
And yet he says that *'it pleases him well, and that it is profitable and necessary.'*

But he does not say it to be necessary to all but only to pacify troubled consciences, as I suppose.

Thus, Luther lets it be understood that if anyone with a conscience like his - which is either *safe by his own sanctity* or assured by the word of the divine promise - has no need to confess his secret sins at all.

Otherwise, a scrupulous person may confess his sins to calm his conscience.

Therefore, seeing he has left his words suspended in doubt, I will speak more plainly of the necessity of Confession.

Since Luther denies confession of secret sins to be proved by Scripture, I will, in the first place, propose that passage in Ecclesiastics which seems to many – myself included - to comprehend all three parts of Penance.

'My Son, in thy sickness, neglect not thyself, but pray to the Lord, and He shall heal thee. Turn away from sin and order thy hands aright, and cleanse thy heart from all offence.' (Eccl. 38:9-10)

Because God cures, while He looses in heaven what the priest has loosed on earth. [64]

We lift up our hands in satisfaction; we turn from our sins by contrition. In confession, we cleanse our hearts from sin, according to that saying of the prophet, *'pour out your hearts before Him'* (Ps. 61:9).

St. John Chrysostom also comprehends the three parts of penance, when he says, *'Perfect penance compels the sinner to endure all things willingly.'* And further he says, *'Contrition in his heart, confession in his mouth, a perfect humility in his works; this is fruitful penance.'*

This also makes for Confession: *'be diligent to know the countenance of thy cattle, and consider thy own flocks'* (Prov. 27:23).

But how can one know it, if it is not shown him? [65]

What is clearer than that is found in the fifth chapter of Numbers? *'The Lord spoke to Moses, saying: say to the children of Israel: When a man or woman shall have committed any of all the sins that men are wont*

---

[64] The first and chief sacrament for the forgiveness of sins is Baptism. For those sins committed after Baptism, Christ instituted the sacrament of Reconciliation or Penance through which a baptized person is reconciled with God and with the Church (Compendium, Number 200).

[65] Each of the faithful who has reached the age of discretion is bound to confess his or her mortal sins at least once a year and always before receiving Holy Communion (*Compendium*, Number 305).

to commit, and by negligence shall have transgressed the commandment of the Lord, and offended, they shall confess their sin' (Num. 5:5-7).

This, too, is part of the old Jewish Law, which had all things in figure: it commanded those infected with leprosy to *show themselves to the priest.*

God has therefore written in the Law, *'thou shalt not muzzle the ox that treadeth out thy corn on the floor'* (Deut. 25:4).

Thus, He admonishes us that it is just that he who serves at the altar should live by the altar, as the Apostle declares, saying, *'it is written in the Law of Moses: thou shalt not muzzle the mouth of the ox that treadeth out the corn. Doth God take care for oxen'* (1Cor 9:9)?

There is no reason to doubt that, in the Law of the flesh, the leprosy of the body was a figure of sin in the spiritual Law.

And Christ, in order that He might bring us to the gradual understanding of this, said to the lepers whom He cleansed - not only from the leprosy of the body, but also of the soul - *'go show yourselves to the priest'* (Lk. 17:14) and that verse of St. James also, *'confess your sins to one another'* (Jas 5:16). [66]

I am not ignorant of the various interpretations given by many to this passage. However, I am of the view, and many more besides me, that it commanded sacramental Confession. [67]

Or does not that saying of Our Lord through Isaias manifestly confirm confession, *'tell if thou hast any thing to justify thyself?'* (Is. 43:26).

If the authority of the Fathers deserves any credit, surely it deserves it in this.

St. Ambrose says, *'no man can be justified from sin, if he does not confess his sin'*. What can be more plainly spoken?

Moreover, St John Chrysostom says, *'he cannot receive the grace of God unless he is cleansed from all his sins by confession'*.

---

[66] It requires that we admit our faults and repent of our sins. God himself by his Word and his Spirit lays bare our sins and gives us the truth of conscience and the hope of forgiveness (*Compendium*, Number 391).

[67] Christ has entrusted the ministry of Reconciliation to his apostles, to the bishops who are their successors and to the priests who are the collaborators of the bishops, all of whom become thereby instruments of the mercy and justice of God. They exercise their power of forgiving sins in the name of the Father and of the Son and of the Holy Spirit (*Compendium*, Number 307).

Lastly, St. Augustine: *'do penance, such as is done in the Church. Let no man say to himself, 'I do it secretly because I do it with God'. It that were true, without reason it was said, 'I will give to thee the keys of the kingdom of heaven' (Mt 16:19) and 'whatsoever you shall loose upon earth shall be loosed upon earth (Mt 18:18)'.*

Even if we suppose that not one word was written about confession, either explicitly or figuratively, nor anything spoken of it by the holy Fathers, we would still have to consider the fact that all people have confessed their sins to the priests for so many ages.

When I consider the good that continually follows its practice, and no evil at all, I cannot possibly believe that it was established or upheld by any human invention.

I believe it was established by the divine Order of God.

Because no human authority could ever induce the people to reveal their secret sins, which, in their consciences, they abhor and are so greatly concerned to keep hidden in shame and confusion - much less to a man (the priest) who might reveal them when he pleased. [68]

Because since God Himself, the Author of the Sacrament, defends this wholesome practice by His special grace, it could not happen that among such great numbers of priests, some good, some bad, indifferently hearing confessions, they should all retain them; especially when some of them can keep nothing else secret.

For my part, let Luther say what he will.

I will believe that Confession was instituted and is preserved by God Himself and not by any custom of the people, or institution of the Fathers. [69]

Luther condemns the reservation of some sins, whereby a particular priest is prevented from remitting all; but that some sins are not forgiven,

---

[68] Given the delicacy and greatness of this ministry and the respect due to people every confessor, without any exception and under very severe penalties, is bound to maintain *"the sacramental seal"* which means absolute secrecy about the sins revealed to him in confession (Compendium, Number 309).

[69] The risen Lord instituted this sacrament on the evening of Easter when he showed himself to his apostles and said to them, *"Receive the Holy Spirit. If you forgive the sins of any, they are forgiven; if you retain the sins of any, they are retained."* (John 20:22-23) – (*Compendium*, Number 298).

except by the hand of a bishop, and some by the hand of the Pope himself. [70]

This shows how this *popular man* so levels all things so that, through the hatred he bears to the Pope, he casts all other bishops into the rank of the lowest priest.

He is so blinded with malice that he cannot distinguish Jurisdiction from Order.

Nay, he is so blind that he cannot see any Order at all, but rather mingles and confounds all things with horror, and reduces priests themselves into the rank of laymen.

Seeing that God has formed His Church Militant after the example of the Church Triumphant, why doesn't Luther, seeing so many degrees and orders in the Triumphant, admit in the Militant any degree, order, or difference at all?

Why, then, has the Apostle written so much of bishops, if a bishop has no more power over his flock than any other priest or layman? [71]

But we will speak of the laity hereafter. Let us now speak of priests.

Although every priest has Orders, and is deemed to be a fit person to judge anything in Confession, he does not have the authority to do so unless a bishop assigns him to a certain flock. [72]

If the bishop, who has care of the whole diocese, commits any part of his care to a priest, does not reason teach us that the priest can bind or loose only what the bishop has permitted him? [73]

---

[70] The absolution of certain particularly grave sins (like those punished by excommunication) is reserved to the Apostolic See or to the local bishop or to priests who are authorized by them. Any priest, however, can absolve a person who is in danger of death from any sin and excommunication (*Compendium*, Number 308).

[71] Episcopal ordination confers the fullness of the sacrament of Holy Orders. It makes the bishop a legitimate successor of the apostles and integrates him into the Episcopal college to share with the Pope and the other bishops care for all the churches. It confers on him the offices of teaching, sanctifying, and ruling (*Compendium*, Number 326).

[72] A priest, although ordained for a universal mission, exercises his ministry in a particular Church. This ministry is pursued in sacramental brotherhood with other priests who form the "presbyterate". In communion with the bishop, and depending upon him, they bear responsibility for the particular Church (*Compendium*, Number 329).

For without the bishop's authority, he could not have bound or loosed anything at all among the people.

For the same reason it is not lawful for a bishop to act in another Diocese.

Why wonder, then, why a bishop - learned as he is and whose care is greater than what might be assigned to any person - reserves some things to himself, as has been observed for so many ages?

He might do so out of concern that the people might fall more prone to sin, if the power of remission were to be too easily proposed to them.

Now at last, Luther commands everything to be permitted to every person, so that the difficulty of penance may not deter anybody from sin.

He commands thus not only to priests, but also to the laity.

Nay, Luther comes to that height of madness as to suggest that men should go to women to have them hear their confessions, although women are commonly regarded as being unable to conceal anything secret!

I suppose that Luther will not make a woman priest since the Apostle does not permit women to teach - and Luther himself denies almost anyone who is not a preacher to be a priest. [74]

The sentiments of the holy Fathers declare that we ought to confess our sins only to priests, unless otherwise forced by necessity: *'let him come,* (says St. Augustine) *to the priests, who can administer to him the keys of the Church.'*

He does not say, *'let him come to laymen'* or *'let him come to women'*.

In another place, he further tells us the same thing more plainly: *'He that repents, let him truly repent; let him signify his grief by tears; let him present his life to God by the priest; let him prevent the judgment of God by confession. For the Lord commanded them that should be cleansed, that they should show themselves to the Priest.'*

---

[73] The bishop to whom the care of a particular Church is entrusted is the visible head and foundation of unity for that Church. For the sake of that Church, as Vicar of Christ, he fulfils the office of shepherd and is assisted by his own priests and deacons (*Compendium*, Number 327).

[74] This sacrament can only be validly received by a baptized man. The Church recognises herself as bound by this choice made by the Lord Himself. No one can demand to receive the sacrament of Holy Orders, but must be judged suitable for the ministry by the authorities of the Church (*Compendium*, Number 333).

By this we are taught that sins are to be confessed by a bodily presence. [75]

Likewise Pope Leo said: *'Christ gave this power to the governors of the Church, that they should give the satisfaction of penance to them that confess.'*

Further, as the venerable Bede says, *'let us discover our light and daily crimes to our co-equals, and our grievous sins to the priest; and as long as they have dominion in us, let us take care to purge them; for sins cannot be forgiven without confession.'*

Moreover, what should confession avail us, if, by the keys of the Church, absolution did not follow?

'This power (says St. Ambrose) *is given only to Priests.'*

In another place, he declares what the sense of these words is, when he says, *'the words of God remit sin, the priest is judge'*. [76]

Likewise St. Augustine, in another place, writes most plainly, saying, *'he that does penance, without the appointment of the priest, frustrates the keys of the Church.'*

Now let anyone judge the truth of Luther's opinion, who, contrary to the sentiments of all the holy Fathers, draws the keys of the Church to the laity and to women, and says that these words of Christ, *'whatsoever you shall bind,'* etc., are not spoken only to priests, but also to all the faithful.

Marcus Aemilius Scaurus was a most excellent man and of known honesty. He was accused to the people in Rome by Varius Sucronensis, a man of little sincerity.

His accuser made a long and tedious discourse, but Scaurus, confidently relying on the judgment of the people and not thinking that Varius was worthy of an answer, said:

'Romans, Varius Sucronensis says it, Aemilius Scaurus denies it; which of these do you believe?'

---

[75] All grave sins not yet confessed, which a careful examination of conscience brings to mind, must be brought to the sacrament of Penance. The confession of serious sins is the only ordinary way to obtain forgiveness (*Compendium*, Number 304).

[76] The Church has the mission and the power to forgive sins because Christ himself has conferred it upon her: *"Receive the Holy Spirit, if you forgive the sins of any, they are forgiven; if you retain the sins of any, they are retained"* (John 20:22-23) – (*Compendium*, Number 201).

At these words, the people, applauding this honourable man, scorned the idle accusations of his babbling adversary.

Now this discourse does not seem more applicable to them than to us: For Luther says that the words of Christ concerning the keys are spoken to the laity. St. Augustine denies it.

Which of them is rather to be believed?

Luther affirms it; Bede denies it; which of them will you believe?

Luther affirms it; St. Ambrose denies it; which of them has the greatest credit?

Finally, Luther affirms it, and the whole Church denies it: which do you think is to be believed?

If anybody is as mad as to side with Luther that he ought to confess his sins to a woman, perhaps he will also agree with that other opinion of Luther: that we are not be too careful in calling to mind our sins.

Surely, a penitent will not be inclined, in examining his memory, to freely speak into such a person's ear, she who has so large and passable a road from her ear to her tongue.

If there was no such danger, I shall prefer, instead of the counsel of Luther, the example of the prophet, who says, *'I will recount to thee all my years in the bitterness of my soul'* (Is 38:15).

All my years, and that in bitterness.

For such a confession, not only cleanses from sins past, but also abundantly begets new grace, according to that saying of St. Ambrose:

'St. Peter became more faithful after he bewailed the loss of his Faith; and so he obtained a grace greater than that he had lost.' [77]

St. Gregory, following him, says, *'life, which is fervent in love after sin, is much more acceptable to God, than innocence that is sluggish in security.'*

Luther calls idle people those who believe that the circumstances of sin are to be confessed.

See how much St. Augustine differs from him in this, when he says:

---

[77] The effects of the sacrament of Penance are: reconciliation with God and therefore the forgiveness of sins; reconciliation with the Church; recovery, if it has been lost, of the state of grace; remission of the eternal punishment merited by mortal sins, and remission, at least in part, of the temporal punishment which is the consequence of sin; peace, serenity of conscience and spiritual consolation; and an increase of spiritual strength for the struggle of Christian living (*Compendium*, Number 310).

'Let him consider the quality of the crime; as to the place, time, perseverance, distinction of persons, and with what temptation it was done, and how often the sin was committed?

'A fornicator ought to repent according to the excellence of his state, or affairs, and according to the quality of the person with whom he has sinned.

'He ought to repent according to the crime itself - if in a sacred place, in time of prayer, as holy days, and times of fasting.

'He is to consider how long he persisted in sin, and let his sorrow be according to his perseverance in sin; by what assault he was overcome - for there are some, who, far from being overcome, do voluntarily offer themselves to sin; nor do they stay for temptation, but prevent the pleasure.

'Let him consider with what pleasure, and how often, he has committed the sin.

'All these circumstances are to be confessed and bewailed; that when he has known his sin, he may soon find God propitious to him.

'In pondering the weight of his offences, let him consider of what age he is, of what understanding, and order.

'Let him ponder each of these singly, and examine the manner of the crime, purging with tears every quality of the vice.'

Hearing the words of St. Augustine, how can Luther think that circumstances do not appertain to confession?

Who has more diligently reckoned up the circumstances of sins than this holy man has, St Augustine?

I doubt whether Luther will find any one whom he calls idle.

But, if we are to diligently call to mind the various circumstances of sin, how much more are heinous and different crimes to be collected and our conscience diligently to be examined, that, if possible, we may not let one sin escape our knowledge?

Luther darts this phrase as a keen shaft, *'nobody can possibly confess all his sins, because no one can remember them all'*.

This is indeed a very obtuse argument: for who does not know that none of those who said, all sins are to be confessed, was ever so stupid as to think that a man must tell the priest in his ear what he could not remember?

Chapter IX

Of Satisfaction

I DO NOT KNOW how Luther will satisfy others concerning satisfaction. For my part, I think that he should remain silent, rather than choosing to speak many things of no significance at all.

In the first place, he says that *'the Church teaches satisfaction in such a manner that the people can never understand true satisfaction, which is a renovation of life.'*

Who does not see that statement to be a calumny?

Who taught Luther that the Church does not teach that we ought to renew our lives?

He has not travelled over the whole Church or been present at all confessions to hear this ignorance of the priests.

He must *have the Holy Ghost in his bosom* then - or some devil in his breast - which has inspired this into him.

But whatsoever spirit this is, it could not be a good one that taught him a lie.

It had to be that spirit, the devil, of whom it is said to be *'a liar, and the father thereof'* (Jn 8:44).

Everyone knows that what Luther affirms to be true, is really false. Who was ever so doltish as to enjoin - for past sins - satisfactory works that indulged the future?

Who is he who does not continually pronounce these words of Christ, *'go, and now sin no more'* (John 8:11) when he absolves?

And those words of St. Paul, *'as you have yielded your members to serve uncleanness and iniquity, unto iniquity; so now yield your members to serve justice unto sanctification'* (Rom 6:19).

Who has not read the words of St. Gregory: *'we are not able to perform our penance as we ought to, unless we know the manner of the same penance?'*

To do penance is to bewail our formerly committed sins, and resolve not to do anything that we should have cause to sorrow for hereafter. [78]

For he that laments the past so as to commit again in the future does not know how to perform penance, but rather evades it.

What avails it to anybody to grieve for his sins of lust, and yet to burn with covetousness?

Even if nothing of this were mentioned, yet seeing that the priest imposes penance for sins committed, it shows that the sin is not to be committed again. If it is, it must be punished again.

It is therefore very evident that Luther has no regard to what he says, as long as he may say something that may slander the Church.

This appears to be so wherever he cries aloud, as in some matter of great moment, as he does in these words:

'What monstrous things are we indebted to thee, thou See of Rome! And to thy murderous laws and rites, whereby thou hast so destroyed the

---

[78] [Interior penance] is the movement of a *"contrite heart"* (Psalm 51:19) drawn by divine grace to respond to the merciful love of God. This entails sorrow for and abhorrence of sins committed, a firm purpose not to sin again in the future and trust in the help of God. It is nourished by hope in divine mercy (*Compendium*, Number 300).

whole world, that people think they can by works satisfy God for their sins. When nothing but only the Faith of a contrite heart can satisfy Him.

' *By these tumults thou not only puttest to silence, but even oppressest, only that thine insatiable blood-suckers may have people to say to them, 'bring, bring, that you may sell sins'!"*

Who would not think, by reading these so furious and tragic words, that Luther had discovered some great and abominable prodigy in the Roman See?

But anyone who diligently examines all these things will see that *'the mountains brought forth a ridiculous mouse.'*

First of all, how ridiculous is that exclamation of his against the See of Rome?

As if works of satisfaction were exacted and penance imposed only at Rome, and not through the whole Church in all parts of the world?

Or, as if many of the laws – which Luther calls *murderous laws* – had not been ordained by the Holy Fathers in former times, by Synods, General Councils and the public consent of all Christians?

Finally, Luther says that *'we cannot satisfy God by works, but by faith alone'.*

If he meant that by works alone, without faith, we cannot do it, he shows his folly by railing against the See of Rome.

Because Rome, aware of the teaching of Saint Paul - *'all that is not of faith is sin'* (Rom. 14:23) - has never said that works, without faith, can satisfy. It would have been foolish to say so.

If he thinks that works are superfluous, and that faith alone is sufficient, whatever the works may be, then he does say something, and truly dissents from the Roman Church which, with St James, believes that *'faith, if it have not works, is dead in itself'* (Jas. 2:17-20).

You see how impertinently Luther troubles himself, by so furiously inveighing against the See of Rome, so as to ensnare himself in folly and impiety in the meanwhile.

I think it is more probable, indeed, that Luther is of the opinion that Faith, without good works, is always sufficient for salvation.

It evidently appears that he is of that opinion, as by this saying, *'God does nothing regarding our works, not has any need of them; but He has need that we should believe Him true in His promises'*; and others of his passages.

Luther knows best what he meant by these words.

For my part, I believe that God cares for our Faith and our works, and that He needs neither our Faith nor our works.

Although God has no need of our goods, He cares so much about what we do that He commands some things to be done, and forbids others.

Without His care, not so much as one sparrow falls to the earth, *'five of which are sold for two farthings'* (Lk 12:6).

But since Luther urges that a penitent ought only to renew his life and neglect to undergo any penance from the priest for his past sins, let us hear what St. Augustine has written on this subject:

'It is not sufficient to change our manners for the better and forsake our former wickedness, unless we also do satisfy Our Lord for the sins committed by the sorrows of penance; by the sobs of humility; by the sacrifice of a contrite heart with the cooperation of alms, deeds and fasts.'

And in another place, he says, *'Let the penitent deliver himself altogether unto the judgement and power of the priest, reserving nothing of himself to himself, that he may be ready to do all things as he is commanded towards recovering the life of the soul; which he should do to avoid the death of the body.'*

Likewise, in another place, *'the priests do also bind when they enjoin the satisfaction of penance to those who come to confession. They loose when they remit anything of it.'*

'They exercise a work of justice towards sinners, when they bind them with just punishment; it is a work of mercy which they remit somewhat of the same punishment.'

I hope I have made clear how rashly Luther calumniates the Church, and, through the whole Sacrament of Penance, how impertinent, how impious, and how absurd he is against the holy Fathers; against Scriptures; against the public faith of the Church; against the consent of so many ages and people; even against common sense itself.

Still, he is not yet content with all of that; after having held for a long time that Penance is a Sacrament, he began to change his mind at the end of his book, lest it could contain anything true at all.

Therefore, as his custom is, he changes his opinion into a worse one, and wholly denies Penance to be a Sacrament.

He confessed before that *'he does not doubt, but that whoever, of his own accord, or by reproofs, has privately confessed himself before any brother, and demanded pardon, and amended himself, is absolved from all his secret sins.'*

If this is his sentiment, it is false indeed.

Because he says, *'before any brother privately, and that indifferently; whether he asks pardon of his own accord or as forced to it by rebukes'.*

If, I say, he thinks such a penance to be profitable, why does he exclude it from the number of the Sacraments?

He does not do so for any other intent, except that it may be less valued.

Thus, being deprived of the name of a Sacrament, which among Christians is in great veneration, Penance might become despicable.

Thus, he find no other pretext but that Penance has no visible sign, as though the exterior penance, or the very act and gestures of the body, when the priest absolves the penitent, could not be a sign of spiritual grace, whereby the penitent obtains remission. [79]

But, in fine, to conclude the discourse on Penance, I wish he may at last repent himself for having treated of Penance in so evil a manner, that he may wholesomely perform all its parts, since he endeavours to destroy them all; that he may be contrite for his malice and publicly confess his errors; and, that by submitting himself to the judgement of the Church – which he has offended with so many blasphemies – he may atone for what he has previously committed with the greatest satisfaction possible, for indeed he cannot do it worthily.

---

[79] Penance can be expressed in many and various ways but above all in fasting, prayer, and almsgiving. These and many other forms of penance can be practiced in the daily life of a Christian, particularly during the time of Lent and on the penitential day of Friday (*Compendium*, Number 301).

Chapter X

Of Confirmation

LUTHER is so FAR from admitting Confirmation to be a Sacrament that, on the contrary, he is *'amazed at what the Church's intention was in making it one.'*

Here is how this most impertinent babbler trifles in so sacred a thing: he asks why the Church does not make three Sacraments of bread, since She has some occasions to do it in Scripture.

The Church has not done any such thing.

She has no other Sacraments than those instituted by Christ and sanctified by His most holy Blood.

She takes no occasions from any words whatsoever in Scripture for having any other.

Likewise, the Church omits none of those that have been given by Christ and his Apostles and transmitted to us, as it were, from hand to hand, even though nothing had been written of them anywhere. [80]

But when he says that *'Confirmation works no salvation'* and that it is not supported by any promise of Christ, he proves nothing. He only says it, while denying all.

When Luther makes mention of some passages, from which (though he laughs at it) the Sacrament of Confirmation probably had its beginning, why does he judge the whole Church so perversely, as if She should rashly admit a Sacrament? [81]

He reads no word of promise in these places, as if Christ had promised, said, or done nothing except what the Evangelists mention in the Scriptures!

By this rule, if there had been no Gospel but that of St. John, he should deny the Institution of the Sacrament of our Lord's Supper, since St. John writes nothing at all about this institution.

Many other things done by Jesus have been omitted by all, which, as the Evangelist himself says *'but there are also many other things which Jesus did which, if they were written every one, the world itself, I think, would not be able to contain the books that should be written'* (John 21:25).

Some of these things have been delivered to the faithful by the mouth of the Apostles. The perpetual Faith of the Holy Catholic Church has

---

[80] Apostolic Tradition is the transmission of the message of Christ, brought about from the very beginnings of Christianity by means of preaching, bearing witness, institutions, worship, and inspired writings. The apostles transmitted all they received from Christ and learned from the Holy Spirit to their successors, the bishops, and through them to all generations until the end of the world (*Compendium*, Number 12).

[81] In the Old Testament the prophets announced that the Spirit of the Lord would rest on the awaited Messiah and on the entire messianic people. The whole life and mission of Jesus were carried out in total communion with the Holy Spirit. The apostles received the Holy Spirit at Pentecost and proclaimed *"the great works of God"* (Acts 2:11). They gave the gift of the same Spirit to the newly baptized by the laying on of hands. Down through the centuries, the Church has continued to live by the Spirit and to impart him to her children (*Compendium*, Number 265).

safeguarded them ever after. I think you ought to believe Her concerning some things which are not in the Gospels.

As St. Augustine says, *'you could never know which is the Scripture itself, but by the Tradition of the Church'.*

Even if no book had ever been written, the Gospel would have remained always written in the hearts of the faithful, which is more ancient than all the Books of the Evangelists.

Let Luther not think that by not finding the Sacraments instituted in the Scriptures, he has a prevailing argument to prove their nullity.

So that he may have no cause for wrangling, I say: since he admits nothing at all but what he reads clearly in the Gospel, how does he come to believe the perpetual Virginity of the Blessed Virgin Mary - if he believes it, for he scarcely believes anything at all?

He is so far from finding anything about it in Scripture that Helvidius took occasion to argue the contrary by Scripture itself.

Luther has nothing to oppose him except the Faith of the whole Church, which is nowhere greater and stronger than in the Sacraments.

Christ prayed for St. Peter that *his Faith should not fail* (Lk 22:32), and *placed His Church on a firm Rock.*

For my part, I do not think that any one who has the least spark of Faith in him can be persuaded that he should expect her, for so many ages, to be bound by vain signs of bodily things under an erroneous confidence of their being divine Sacraments.

Even if nothing should be read of it anywhere, yet those who were present and conversed with our Lord could tell what His Mind was by word of mouth.

He Himself says of them, *'you shall give testimony, because you are with Me from the beginning'* (John 15:27).

What was to be done could have been taught by the Holy Ghost, of Whom Christ said, *'but when the Paraclite cometh, Whom I will send you from the Father, the Spirit of Truth, Who proceedeth from the Father, He shall give testimony of Me'* (John 15:26).

And in another place: *'when He, the Spirit of Truth, is come, He will teach you all Truth. For He shall not speak of Himself; but what things soever He shall hear, He shall speak; and the things that are to come, He shall show you'* (John 16:13).

Shall we believe then that the Church, having so many and great ministers, so many living Evangelists and that Spirit which inspires truth, has rashly instituted a Sacrament, and put her hope in an empty sign?

Or, rather, shall we believe that She did learn from the Apostles and from the Spirit of Truth? [82]

Certainly, if we consider the name, the minister, and the virtue promised in this Sacrament, it will not appear to be something that we may believe the Church uses unadvisedly.

As Hugo de Saint-Victor says, *'from Chrism is Christ named; from Christ, Christian'*.

Every one ought to have taken Chrism, or unction, since from it they take their common name, because we are all *'a chosen generation, a kingly priesthood'* (1 Pet 2:9) in Christ.

We are only anointed by the Bishops, [83] unless in case of necessity, so that they may seal the Christian and give him the Holy Ghost:

'Even (says he) *as we read that in the early Church only the Apostles had power to give the Holy Ghost by imposition of hands.'*

The same Doctor also declares the fruit of the Sacrament: *'as the remission of sins is received in Baptism; so, is the Holy Ghost given by the imposition of hands.*

'There, grace is given for the remission of sins. Here, grace is given for Confirmation.

'For what avails it to you to be lifted up from your fall, if you are not confirmed to stand?'

These are Hugo's words, which are also consistent with reason.

In the corporal life, we get life by generation. And yet another action is required, whereby we may increase and grow to the perfection of strength.

In the spiritual life, we obtain regeneration by Baptism.

---

[82] The essential rite of Confirmation is the anointing with Sacred Chrism (oil mixed with balsam and consecrated by the bishop), which is done by the laying on of the hand of the minister who pronounces the sacramental words proper to the rite. In the West this anointing is done on the forehead of the baptized with the words, *"Be sealed with the gift of the Holy Spirit"*. In the Eastern Churches of the Byzantine rite this anointing is also done on other parts of the body with the words, *"The seal of the gift of the Holy Spirit"* (*Compendium*, Number 267).

[83] The original minister of Confirmation is the bishop. In this way the link between the confirmed and the Church in her apostolic dimension is made manifest. When a priest confers this sacrament, as ordinarily happens in the East and in special cases in the West, the link with the bishop and with the Church is expressed by the priest who is the collaborator of the bishop and by the Sacred Chrism, consecrated by the bishop himself (*Compendium*, Number 270).

So the Sacrament of Confirmation is necessary, whereby the spiritual life is led to perfect virtue and the Holy Ghost is given for perfect strength. [84]

And besides the Sacrament of Baptism, which helps us to believe, Confirmation is profitable to give us courage boldly to confess our Faith. To this is it so ordained, that man may, before the persecutor, boldly confess his Faith.

This is what Melchiades says:

'In Baptism we are regenerated to life, after Baptism we are confirmed for the combat. Confirmation arms and instructs us against the agonies of this world'.

Finally, we will relate here what St. Jerome has written of this Sacrament of Confirmation in order that Luther may understand that it is neither new nor vain fiction.

In reality, it is so far from being void of grace that it confers the Spirit of Grace and Truth:

'If the Bishop imposes his hand, it is on them who have been baptised in the true Faith, who have believed in the Father, Son, and Holy Ghost, three Persons and one Substance.

Now stop your ears that you may not be polluted with the words of such monstrous impiety of the Arians: 'on the contrary, the Arian believes in no other but in the Father alone, in Jesus Christ as a creature, in the Holy Ghost as servant to both. How shall he receive the Holy Ghost from the Church, he who has not as yet obtained remission of his sins?

'For the Holy Ghost does not indwell except where Faith is pure, nor does He remain anywhere but in that Church which has true Faith for her guide.

'If you ask here, why is it that he who is baptised in the Church does not receive the Holy Ghost except by the hands of the Bishop, learn that this institution is descended from this Authority: after our Lord's Ascension, the Holy Ghost descended on the Apostles, and we find the same to have been done in many places in Scripture'.

This is what St. Jerome says.

---

[84] The effect of Confirmation is a special outpouring of the Holy Spirit like that of Pentecost. This outpouring impresses on the soul an indelible character and produces a growth in the grace of Baptism. It roots the recipient more deeply in divine sonship, binds him more firmly to Christ and to the Church and reinvigorates the gifts of the Holy Spirit in his soul. It gives a special strength to witness to the Christian faith (*Compendium*, Number 268).

What he says is also confirmed by various passages in the Scripture, and particularly in the Acts of the Apostles.

The people that had been baptised before in Samaria received the Holy Ghost when Peter and John came among them, and laid their hands upon them (Acts 8:14-17). [85]

It amazes me how it should come into Luther's mind to dispute that Confirmation is only to be accounted as a rite and a ceremony, and deny it to be a Sacrament.

For it is demonstrated that not only grace, but also the very Spirit of Grace, is conferred by the visible sign of the Bishop's imposition of hands.

This is confirmed not only by the testimony of holy Fathers and by the Faith of the whole Church, but also by clear passages of Scripture.

Let Luther therefore no longer despise the Sacrament of Confirmation, which is commended by the dignity of the minister, the authority of the Church, and the profit of the Sacrament itself.

---

[85] Only those already baptized can and should receive this sacrament which can be received only once. To receive Confirmation efficaciously the candidate must be in the state of grace (Compendium, Number 269).

Chapter XI

Of the Sacrament of Marriage

 ARRIAGE, the first of all Sacraments, celebrated by the first of mankind and honoured with our Saviour's first miracle, has had Sacrament for its very name for so long a time in a religious veneration. [86]

---

[86] God who is love and who created man and woman for love has called them to love. By creating man and woman he called them to an intimate communion of life and of love in marriage: *"So that they are no longer two, but one flesh"*

At last, Luther denies that it is any Sacrament at all, that people should not so much regard or value conjugal faith.

Luther takes away from us some of the other Sacraments, either by denying the presence of the sign or the promised grace.

In Marriage he denies both to be present.

He holds that nowhere has grace been promised thereby, and he also teaches that nowhere has it has been instituted for a sign.

And how does he know this?

'Because (says he) *we read it not'.*

O strong reason and mother of many heresies! This was the fountain from which Helvidius drew his venom.

You admit no Sacrament unless you read its institution in a Book! What Book was ever written that instituted all?

'Concerning some things, (says he) *I believe Christ's Evangelists'.*

Why then doesn't he - in some things - believe also the Church of Christ, which is preferred by Christ Himself to all the Evangelists, who were only members of the Church?

Wherefore, if he trusts so much in one, why does he distrust all together?

If he attributes so much to a member, why does he attribute nothing at all to the whole Body?

The Church believes that it is a Sacrament, instituted by God, given by Christ and left to us by His Apostles.

Afterwards, the Holy Fathers delivered it as a Sacrament and passed on, as it were, from hand to hand to us.

And from us also, as a Sacrament, down to posterity and to be honoured until the end of the world.

The Church believes this, and tells you what She believes too.

The same Church that says, *'the Evangelists wrote the Gospel'*, tells you this also.

If the Church had not said that *'the Gospel of John is the Gospel of John,'* you should not have known it; for you were not present when he wrote it.

Why, then, don't you believe the Church when She tells you that Christ did these things, and instituted these Sacraments, the Apostles delivered them, as well as when she says, *'that the Evangelists wrote such and such Gospels'?*

(Matthew 19:6). God said to them in blessing *"Be fruitful and multiply"* (Genesis 1:28) – (*Compendium*, Number 337).

Luther says, *'Marriage was among the ancient Patriarchs, and among the Gentiles, just as it is among us; yet it was not a Sacrament with either of them.'*

As for the Fathers that were under the Law, and before the Law, I do not agree with Luther. But I am certain that Marriage was a Sacrament with them as well as circumcision.

Among the Gentiles, however, the case is different. Because their marriage depended on the customs and laws of each people, so that some marriages were lawful with some of them, which by others were accounted ridiculous.

And yet, contrary to Luther, we find some of the opinion that even the marriages of the Gentiles were a sacrament among them.

St. Augustine says *'the Sacrament of Marriage is common to all nations: but the sanctity of it is only in the City of our God, and in His holy Mountain'*, the Church.

In this regard, let us read Hugo de Saint-Victor.

But although the marriage of the faithless is no Sacrament, neither does it follow what Luther infers, that the Marriage of the faithful is not.

The people of God have always had something holier in Marriage, as well as having it as its first institution, when it was honoured with the laws given by God. [87]

Moreover, because it was enacted as a human thing among them, the Gentiles were wont to take wives by compacts and human laws, and reject them again afterward.

Divorce was not lawful in former times amongst the People of God: for though God, by Moses, permitted the bill of divorce among the Hebrews, yet Christ declared that it was permitted them because of the hardness of the people's hearts:

'For from the beginning (says our Saviour), *it was not so'.*

Christ has restored Christians to pristine sanctity, consecrating Marriage with an inseparable bond of society - unless in case of

---

[87] God helped his people above all through the teaching of the Law and the Prophets to deepen progressively their understanding of the unity and indissolubility of marriage. The nuptial covenant of God with Israel prepared for and prefigured the new covenant established by Jesus Christ the Son of God, with his spouse, the Church (*Compendium*, Number 340).

fornication - between those whom God Himself, and no human error, has joined together. [88]

It does not follow, therefore, that if Marriage was not a Sacrament among the Gentiles or the ancient Patriarchs, it must not be so among us Christians.

Among Christians, the Faith of the Church ought to suffice us, even if it was written nowhere.

Moreover, that one passage of the Apostle - which Luther endeavours to disregard with a scoff - plainly demonstrates that Marriage was instituted as a Sacrament, not only now, but at the very beginning of mankind.

And I suppose that nobody will doubt this if he reads and attentively considers that part of the Epistle to the Ephesians.

That whole passage we have inserted here because it cannot be explained any more clearly by any man's words, than it has already been explained by the Apostle himself.

He has so plainly shown us his mind in this matter that no place of refuge is left to Luther's impertinent calumnies.

He says, *'Being subject one to another, in the fear of Christ. Let women be subject to their husbands, as to the Lord: Because the husband is the head of the wife, as Christ is the head of the Church. He is the saviour of his body.*

'Therefore as the Church is subject to Christ: so also let the wives be to their husbands in all things.

'Husbands, love your wives, as Christ also loved the church and delivered himself up for it: that he might sanctify it, cleansing it by the laver of water in the word of life: That he might present it to himself, a glorious Church, not having spot or wrinkle or any such thing; but that it should be holy and without blemish.

'So also ought men to love their wives as their own bodies. He that loveth his wife loveth himself. For no man ever hated his own flesh, but nourisheth and cherisheth it, as also Christ doth the Church: Because we are members of him, body, of his flesh and of his bones.

---

[88] Christ not only restored the original order of matrimony but raised it to the dignity of a sacrament, giving spouses a special grace to live out their marriage as a symbol of Christ's love for his bride the Church: *"Husbands, love your wives as Christ loves the Church"* (Ephesians 5:25) – *Compendium*, Number 341).

'For this cause shall a man leave his father and mother: and shall cleave to his wife; and they shall be two in one flesh. This is a great Sacrament: but I speak in Christ and in the Church.' (Eph 5:22 ff).

You see how the blessed Apostle teaches everywhere that the Marriage of man and wife is a Sacrament, which represents the conjunction of Christ with his Church.

He teaches that God consecrated Matrimony to be the mystery of Christ joined with His Church.

He tells you that the man and wife make one body, of which the man is the head; and that Christ and the Church make one Body, of which Christ is the Head.

He makes the main reason as to why the husband must love his wife: so that he may be a sign like unto Christ, whom he represents.

This he makes the cause, rather than that common nature of the male and female, which of itself should also excite love.

By the same example, he *'exhorts the wife to fear and respect her husband,'* because she represents the Church of Christ.

The Apostle inculcates these things over and over again by many words, lest anybody should think this comparison of the husband with Christ - and the wife with the Church - to be some analogy used only for the convenience of the exhortation.

He further shows it to be a true matter, a true Sacrament, foretold by the prophecy of the principal and first of all Prophets, when the world was but newly created.

The Apostle says that *'he that loveth his wife loveth himself. For no man ever hated his own flesh, but nourisheth and cherisheth it, as also Christ doth the church: Because we are members of him, body, of his flesh and of his bones.'*

This he spoke to remind us of the words, much like those words that Adam spoke, when Eve was first brought into his sight: *'this is bone of my bones, and flesh of my flesh.'*

And that the Apostle might more clearly show that the Sacrament of the union of Adam and Eve pertains to that union of Christ with his Church, he added Adam's very words,

'Wherefore a man shall leave father and mother, and shall cleave to his wife: and they shall be two in one flesh.' (Gen. 2:23).

This Sacrament, says the Apostle, *'is great in Christ and the Church'*.

How could he have more evidently refuted Luther than by these words?

Luther impertinently scoffs at them in contending that the Apostle, by saying that *'this Sacrament is great in Christ and his Church'*, had taken away the Sacrament from the Marriage of man and wife.

As if he should deny the Baptism of the body to be a Sacrament, just by saying that the Sacrament of Baptism is great in the washing of the soul.

Or, as if he should deny the species of bread and wine to be a Sacrament, just by saying that the Sacrament of the Eucharist is great in the Body of Christ.

Or, as if he should detract the Sacrament from the Body which He took of the Blessed Virgin, just by saying that the same Sacrament is great in the Mystical Body of Christ.

Who has ever seen any man swell with greater pride for so frivolous a gloss?

Had the Apostle been of this opinion, he would have wanted his words to be interpreted in Luther's way, so as to show that this Sacrament is great only in Christ and His Church, without any reference at all to the Marriage of man and wife.

In that case, it would lessen the force and weight of all those things whereby he had commended Marriage in that comparison of the two unions.

The words of Adam seem to unite man and wife together in mutual love.

If the Apostle intended his words to refer only to Christ and His Church, it would have prejudiced the matter of which he wrote, teaching that there is no reference to man and wife in them.

The Apostle teaches that those words of Adam were a prophecy of Christ and His Church, which is confirmed by all the holy Doctors.

Further, it also very clearly demonstrates that Adam, by speaking these words at the very first sight of Eve, indicated that man was to leave father and mother and cleave to his wife.

He was not yet referring to the command of begetting children, but instructing man on what father and mother were, by the comparison of parents and children.

If those words of Adam were a prophecy of Christ and His Church, then it seems they either did not belong to that Marriage which was there performed, or that God Himself made a Sacrament of some Marriage as a proper sign of their union.

God's Spirit formed the words of Adam so that the same words might signify both what was then done, and what was prophesied; that is, the Marriage of men and the union of Christ with the Church.

And, as one Sacrament, it comprehends a sacred thing, and the proper and sacred sign of the same thing.

Moreover, in order that you may more clearly perceive that what Luther speaks of is devoid of purpose, observe that the Apostle's purpose in the Epistle to the Ephesians is not about teaching them how great is the Sacrament that Christ joined with the Church.

Instead, it is about exhorting married people how to behave themselves one towards another, so that they may render their Marriage a Sacrament like - and agreeable to - that so sacred a thing which the Sacrament is.

Luther either reads this passage unadvisedly, is negligent, or else he most impiously dissembles any truth he discovers in it.

He says, *'that which we give,* (which is the understanding of the whole Church) *proceeds from great idleness, negligence and inconsiderate reading of it.'*

Does St. Augustine therefore read the Apostle carelessly?

Has St. Jerome, and indeed all men, understood him negligently?

Was it Luther alone, who, by his *vigilance*, discovered St. Paul to have written of Marriage not as a Sacrament, but as a mystery?

O this *quick-sighted* man! He who claims that the whole Latin Church wrongfully names Marriage a Sacrament, whereas the Apostle - when writing in Greek - calls it *Mystery*, and not *Sacrament!*

As if the Latins had erred by speaking the word in Latin, because St. Paul does not use a Latin word in the Greek tongue.

If the interpreter, from this passage of the Apostle, had translated the word as *Mystery* instead of *Sacrament*, and had left the Greek word unchanged; this would not have weakened the argument that Marriage is concluded to be a Sacrament.

The context of the whole matter shows it to be so taught.

Let him wrest the word Mystery as much as he will; by it he can never take away, nor deny, the Sacrament, even though it may not be proved thereby.

No one will be accused of thinking or speaking ill who says that the Eucharist is a great Mystery, for there is no Sacrament that is not a Mystery; that is, a visible sign which contains a hidden and invisible grace.

Thus, the interpreter notes, in the words of St. Paul to the Ephesians, that the whole passage most evidently declares that the Apostle writes of such a Mystery as a real Sacrament.

And if he had not truly translated it, St. Augustine and St. Jerome, his readers, were not so careless that they did not discover the errors in the translation.

Nor did they favour Marriage so much as to continue an error rather than correct it, when once discovered.

This is especially so, seeing that St. Augustine was not inferior to Luther in the knowledge of the Greek tongue.

Also St. Jerome, who, without a doubt, was the most skilled of his time in that language, did so favour virginity that, by some persons, he was thought to be almost unjust towards Marriage.

Therefore, so that all men may more easily understand not only these - whom Luther contemptuously calls *sententious and idle* readers - but also the best and most learned of the ancient Fathers of the Church, let us hear what St. Augustine says:

'Not only fecundity, whose fruit is in the offspring; not only in chastity, whose bond is faith, but also the Sacrament of Marriage, is commended to the faithful, married people. 'For this reason, the Apostle says, husbands, love your wives, as Christ also loved the Church and delivered Himself up for it'(Eph 5:25).

St. Augustine, then, calls it a Sacrament, and, so that Luther may not say he has read this passage carelessly, St. Augustine treats of the same text, again and again, in various works. [89]

In another place, he says, *'it has been said in paradise, man shall leave father and mother, and cleave to his wife (Gen 2:24), which is called by the Apostle a great Sacrament in Christ and His Church'.*

Seeing that in the Greek text St. Paul calls it Mystery, not Sacrament, why does not St. Augustine explain that mystery of Luther's - which the Latins call a Sacrament - to be an error?

St. Augustine, over a thousand times, calls it *the Sacrament of Marriage*; as in that place where he says, *'that offspring, faith, and*

---

[89] The sacrament of Matrimony establishes a perpetual and exclusive bond between the spouses. God himself seals the consent of the spouses. Therefore, a marriage which is ratified and consummated between baptized persons can never be dissolved. Furthermore, this sacrament bestows upon the spouses the grace necessary to attain holiness in their married life and to accept responsibly the gift of children and provide for their education (*Compendium*, Number 346).

Sacrament, which are all the goodness of Marriage, are fulfilled in the parents of Christ Himself".

Why has he not admonished us here that it is not a Sacrament, but a Mystery?

If what Luther says is true – that Marriage is not a Sacrament, but only concerns Christ and His Church – then what Saint Augustine says is not true.

If that which Luther takes as being only a mystery is not the good Sacrament of Marriage, then it was not fulfilled in the Marriage of the Virgin Mary.

And in another place, St. Augustine, addressing the same words of the Apostle, says, *'what is great in Christ and the Church is very little in man and wife; and yet, it is an inseparable Sacrament of conjunction'*.

Luther holds that it is not called a Sacrament, unless in Christ and His Church; but the Apostle's very words shall convince him, if diligently examined only by a Grammarian. The Apostle says, *'this Sacrament is great, but I say in Christ and the Church'*.

What Sacrament is that, that is great in Christ and the Church?

Christ and the Church cannot be a Sacrament in Christ and the Church. Nobody speaks like this.

It is therefore a necessary consequence that this Sacrament, which he says is great in Christ and the Church, is that conjunction of man and wife, of which he has spoken.

There is nothing else but this spoken here by the Apostle, that is, *'this conjunction of man and woman is a great Sacrament in Christ and the Church, as a sacred sign in a most sacred thing.'*

Lastly, if Luther still obstinately denies that, by the words of the Apostle, Marriage should be called a Sacrament, but merely the union of Christ with the Church; yet he will surely not deny that the union of man and wife is at least a sign of that sacred union of Christ and His Church. And, that is also true by God's own institution, not by human invention, seeing that God Himself joined our first parents. [90]

---

[90] The marital union of man and woman, which is founded and endowed with its own proper laws by the Creator, is by its very nature ordered to the communion and good of the couple and to the generation and education of children. According to the original divine plan this conjugal union is indissoluble, as Jesus Christ affirmed: *"What God has joined together, let no man put asunder"* (Mark 10:9) – *Compendium*, Number 338).

But if he denies all this that has been said, the Apostle's words will, however, reveal his impudence. It is repeated so often and so plainly that he who does not see it must undoubtedly confess himself to be blind.

Therefore, since it evidently appears that grace is conferred by Marriage - which is a sign of a thing so sacred - Luther will be compelled - whether he wills it or not - to admit that Marriage is a Sacrament.

Otherwise, he rejects all Sacraments, since, by his own admission a Sacrament consists in the sign of a sacred thing, and the promise of grace.

Let us see then, if it can be made evident that grace is infused by Marriage in any way, for Luther flatly denies it.

'We read in no place, (says he) *that he who marries a wife shall receive any grace from God.'*

But *'marriage* (says the Apostle) *is honourable in all, and the bed undefiled'* (Heb 13:4).

If Marriage lacked grace, the bed could not be undefiled, and Marriage would have nothing else to confer.

God's bounty has provided that no necessary thing should be wanting even to irrational creatures, according to their several natures and capacities; nay, even to things lacking sense.

He has, by the same bountiful Providence, joined grace to Marriage, whereby he who does not slight it but keeps his Faith inviolate to his wife, shall not contract any blemish by the carnal act – which, by its unclean concupiscence, would otherwise stain him.

Nay, on the contrary, he shall be advanced to Grace.

Marriage would not have an immaculate bed if the grace that is infused by it did not turn into good what should be otherwise a sin.

This is more plainly demonstrated in another passage of St. Paul, where he treats of the woman's duty: *'she shall be saved through child bearing'* (1 Tim 2:15).

But if you take away the Sacrament in Marriage, what else shall generation be, but death and eternal damnation?

'If you take away marriage (says St. Bernard) *and an undefiled bed from the Church, do you not then fill it with adultery, incest, sodomy, and all sorts of uncleanness?'*

If all generation out of wedlock is damnable, the grace of Marriage must be truly great, whereby that act is not only purged to take away the blemish, but is so much sanctified that it becomes meritorious, as the Apostle testifies.

Marriage has that privilege of grace by virtue of the Sacrament, consecrated for that purpose by God Himself, so that man, at his first creation, might, by the use of it, perform both his duty of propagation and also have a remedy for concupiscence after the fall.

What should the conjugal act itself be but concupiscence, if God had not made it its remedy?

The holy grace of the Sacrament has made a remedy for concupiscence so that the paternal substance may not be negligently consumed, as the prodigal son had done, forbidding not only, not to thirst after stolen waters of other men's cisterns, but also not to inebriate ourselves with our own.

Rather, we make our sober draughts so wholesome that they may profit to life everlasting.

Although the Apostle exhorted as much as possible to continence and virginity, virtues different from conjugal generation, he acknowledged in the same place that Marriage is the gift of God, and one of those gifts of which it is said, *'every best gift and every perfect gift is from above, coming down from the Father of lights'* (Jas 1:17).

The gift of God is certainly given so that he who receives it may continue in that state of life in which he ought to remain, and not fall into the state of destruction.

Now, does it not show that the gift has in itself safeguarding grace?

Moreover, when the Apostle says, *'if any brother hath a wife that believeth not and she consent to dwell with him: let him not put her away. And if any woman hath a husband that believeth not and he consent to dwell with her: let her not put away her husband.*

'For the unbelieving husband is sanctified by the believing wife: and the unbelieving wife is sanctified by the believing husband. Otherwise your children should be unclean: but now they are holy' (1 Cor. 7:12-14).

Do not these words of the Apostle show that in Marriage - which is an entire thing of itself, after one of the parties is converted to the Faith - the sanctity of the Sacrament sanctifies the whole Marriage, which before was altogether unclean?

Why should that marriage now be holier than before, if, since one of the parties converted, sacramental grace were not added to it?

For Baptism is the door of all the Sacraments, and before it, sacramental grace could not enter into the marriage of the unfaithful.

But, to pass by the Apostle, let us consider God, the Consecrator of this Sacrament.

Has He not consecrated Marriage with His blessing when He joined together our first parents?

For the Scripture says, *'and God blessed them, saying: increase and multiply'* (Gen 1:28), and that blessing operated in all other living creatures, according to their several capacities.

Thus, who would doubt that God has infused the force of spiritual grace into the spirit of man, since man alone is capable of reason?

No one would doubt unless one believes that God, being so bountiful to the meanest of beasts as to largely give them what was necessary according to their natures, should be so sparing of His blessings to man whom He created after His own image.

Who would believe that God, having regard only for man's body, should omit to bestow any part of that great blessing to the soul - that breath of life - which He Himself breathed, and by which He was most represented?

Further, when Christ, God and Man, conversing amongst men, not only honoured Marriage with His own presence, but also adorned it with His first miracle, has He not taught that Marriage is to be honoured?

Without grace, I do not find anything in it deserving honour.

Nor do I think He would have been present at it, if Marriage had not already some grace, which might render it acceptable to Him.

Or else He conferred grace to it Himself.

But I see the miracle that He wrought (John 2) admonishes us that the insipid water of carnal concupiscence is changed to wine of the best taste by the hidden grace of God.

But why do we search so many proofs in so clear a thing?

Especially when that text alone is sufficient for all, where Christ says, *'therefore now they are not two, but one flesh. What therefore God hath joined together, let no man put asunder'* (Mt 19:6).

O the admirable word! Word which none could have spoken, but the Word that was made Flesh!

Who thinks it was not abundantly sufficient that God joined the first of mankind and that the bounty of so great a God is to be admired by all men?

But now we are taught from Truth itself that those who are lawfully married are not rashly joined together.

They are joined not only by the ceremonies of men, but by the invisible Presence and imperceptible co-operation of God Himself.

Therefore, it is forbidden that anyone should separate those whom God has joined together. [91]

O word as full of joy and fears as it is of admiration!

Who should not rejoice that God has so much care over Marriage as to vouchsafe not only to be present at it, but also to preside in it?

Who should not tremble while he is in doubt how to unite to his wife in such a manner, as that he may be able to render her pure and immaculate to God, from Whom he has received her - she whom he is not only bound to love but also to live with?

Therefore, seeing that God himself, as He says, joins all married people together, who does not believe that God infuses grace by Marriage?

Does He join always, and give His blessing but once?

Why does He reassume the office of joining, if we believe Him not also to reassume that of blessing?

Or can we imagine that the most Holy Ghost, *'Who is to be adored in Spirit and in Truth'*, should always exercise the office of joining married people, for the care of bodily union only?

Indeed, as for that matter, it should be sufficient that God leaves man, like other animals, to his own natural and corrupt inclinations.

Therefore, there surely must be understood something holier which God performs in Marriage, than the care of propagating the flesh.

And that, without all doubt, is grace, which is infused into married people by the Prelate of all Sacraments in consecrating Marriage.

Thus, by so many reasons we have proved that grace is conferred in Marriage, and that Marriage, as it appears by the words of the Apostle, is a sign of a sacred thing joined with grace, and therefore cannot be a mere bare figure.

Therefore, it follows that despite Luther, Marriage is a Sacrament. It is referred to by the Apostle as such – even though it had not been called so.

Has anyone, either ancient or modern, doubted to call Marriage a Sacrament, without being hissed at by the Church?

As Hugo de Saint-Victor mentions, in this Sacrament alone is found a two-fold sign:

---

[91] The Church permits the physical separation of spouses when for serious reasons their living together becomes practically impossible, even though there may be hope for their reconciliation. As long as one's spouse lives, however, one is not free to contract a new union, except if the marriage be null and be declared so by ecclesiastical authority (*Compendium*, Number 348).

'Marriage itself is the Sacrament of the society, which is in the Spirit between God and man; but the duty of Marriage is the Sacrament of that society, which in the flesh is between Christ and the Church.

'For if that which is in the flesh is great, much greater is that which is in the Spirit, and if God is rightly called a Bridegroom in Scripture, and the soul of man the bride, there is certainly something between God and the soul of which, what consists between man and woman in Marriage, is the Sacrament and image.

'But perhaps, (to speak more expressly) that society which is outwardly observed according to the contract in Marriage is the Sacrament; and the mutual love of the souls, which is kept by an interchangeable bond of conjugal society and alliance, is the matter of the Sacrament.'

And again, 'this same love, whereby man and woman are spiritually united in the sanctity of wedlock, is the Sacrament and sign of that love. By that love, God is interiorly joined to the rational soul by infusion of His Grace and participation of His Spirit.'

These are the words of Hugo.

Therefore, we have seen that not only the public Faith of the Church for so many ages before us have valued Marriage as a Sacrament, but also the ancient Fathers, remarkable for their virtuous lives and knowledge in Scripture, and also the blessed Apostle, St. Paul, Doctor of the Gentiles.

Marriage makes wedlock honourable, and by grace does not only keep the bed undefiled from adultery, but also washes away the stains of lust, turns water into wine, and procures a holy pleasure of abstaining even from lawful pleasures. [92]

I do not grasp what Luther can say to the contrary.

'Unless, As St Bernard says, 'it is because heretics do still, according to their own fancies, strive to exceed others, in endeavouring, with their viperous teeth, to tear in pieces the Sacrament of the Church, as the heart of their Mother.'

---

[92] Adultery [is] opposed to the sacrament of matrimony because [it] contradicts the equal dignity of man and woman and the unity and exclusivity of married love. Other sins include ... divorce which goes against the indissolubility of marriage (*Compendium*, Number 347).

Chapter XII

Of the Sacrament of Orders

IN THE SACRAMENT OF ORDERS, Luther keeps no manner of order, but gathering together from here and there all the treasures of his malice, he pours them out against it.

He shows how well his mind is composed for evil, if his power were answerable to it. He proposes many things, and asserts and affirms the worst.

But, satisfying himself by only saying this and that, he confirms nothing at all by way of reason.

His great impudence appears in this: Luther, not condescending to believe the whole Church - without knowing the reasons for her faith - unreasonably requires that he himself should be believed, without providing any reason at all.

He requires us to believe him in these matters, but he cannot tell what is to be believed, unless the Church teaches him.

And still he desires to be believed, and in such a manner, as to confound and trample underfoot the whole Church.

For what else does he aim at?

In his endeavour to eliminate the Holy Sacrament of Orders and render the ministers of the Church contemptible, he seeks to persuade the people to despise and undervalue the Sacraments of the Church, as though ministered by the hands of vile and unworthy ministers.

This is the only aim of his whole work. [93]

As Luther proceeds with no order in his treatment of Order, we will gather his opinions here and there, so that the reader may have under one view that heap of evils.

Once that heap has been considered, I suppose that we need not take any great pains to convince him, whose wicked doctrine all men may see tends by infidelity directly to the destruction of the Faith of Christ.

What other design has he, when he argues that...

- There is no difference of priesthood between the laity and priest?
- All men are priests alike?
- All men have the same power, in whatsoever Sacrament?
- The ministry of the Sacraments is not given to the priests but by consent of the laity?
- The Sacrament of Orders is nothing else but the custom of electing a preacher in the Church?
- He who is not a preacher is not a priest, unless it be equivocally said, that a painted man may be called a man?
- A priest may become a layman again, when he pleases, because his priestly character is nothing?

---

[93] Apostolic succession is the transmission by means of the sacrament of Holy Orders of the mission and power of the Apostles to their successors, the bishops. Thanks to this transmission the Church remains in communion of faith and life with her origin, while through the centuries she carries on her apostolate for the spread of the Kingdom of Christ on earth (*Compendium*, Number 176).

Moreover, that the Sacrament of Order itself, which ordains some to be clergymen, is merely and altogether a fiction invented by men, who understand nothing of ecclesiastical matters, of priesthood, of the ministry, of the word, or of a Sacrament?

Finally, this *holy priest* affirms that it is the greatest error and greatest blindness imaginable whereby priests undertake to lead a single life - thus you may conjecture how chaste he himself is.

And when Christ praises those who have made themselves eunuchs for the Kingdom of Heaven, this most filthy Antichrist compares them to the old idolatrous gelded priests of the heathen Sibyls.

I know that this catalogue of pernicious opinions has long since wearied the ears of the pious reader.

Every one of his opinions is more stuffed with heresies than the Trojan horse is reported to have been with armed men.

His denial that Orders is a Sacrament is the fountain to all the rest, as it were: once this fountain is stopped up, the other small springs must of necessity become dry of themselves.

'This Sacrament (says he) *is not known to the Church of Christ, but has been invented by the Church of the Pope'.* In these few words, a great heap of absurdities and lies is contained.

He makes a distinction between the Church of Christ and the Church of the Pope; whereas the Pope is the Vicar of Christ, over whom Christ is the Head.

He says the Church has invented it, whereas She has received it instituted already, and therefore has not invented it.

'This Sacrament (says he) *is unknown to the Church of Christ.'*

On the contrary, it is most certain that all parts of the world that have the true Faith of Christ have Orders for a Sacrament. [94]

Even if Luther could find some obscure corner - which I doubt he can - in which this Sacrament of Orders is not known; yet that corner ought not to be compared to the rest of the whole Church.

The Church is not only subject to Christ, but also to Christ's only Vicar, the Pope of Rome, for the sake of Christ. And the Church believes Orders to be a Sacrament. [95]

---

[94] [Holy orders] is the sacrament through which the mission entrusted by Christ to his apostles continues to be exercised in the Church until the end of time (*Compendium*, Number 322).

[95] Orders designates an ecclesial body into which one enters by means of a special consecration (ordination). Through a special gift of the Holy Spirit, this

Otherwise, if Luther persists in his distinction between the Church of the Pope and that of Christ, and in saying that the one has Orders for a Sacrament, the other not; then let him show us the Church of Christ, which, contrary to the faith of the Papal Church - as he calls Her - does not know the Sacrament of Order.

In the meanwhile, it evidently appears that, by asserting that this Sacrament is unknown to the Church of Christ, Luther affirms that those who are governed by the Pope are not of Christ's Church.

By these two reasons, he separates from the Church of Christ not only Rome, but also all Italy, Germany, Spain, France, Britain, and all other nations that obey the See of Rome or have Orders for a Sacrament.

Now, it consequently follows that since he is removing such people from the Church of Christ, he must confess that either Christ's Church is in no place at all, or else like the Donatists, he must reduce the Catholic Church to two or three heretics whispering in a corner.

He further draws out of his shaft an inevitable dart: that *'grace is in no place promised to this Sacrament;'* and *'that the New Testament does not make the least mention of it; that it is a ridiculous thing to assert that for the Sacrament of God, which nowhere can be demonstrated to have been instituted by God.*

'Nor is it lawful to assert anything to be of Divine institution, which is not of Divine ordinance;

'But we ought to endeavour (says he) *to have all things confirmed to us from clear Scripture.'*

We will see, by and by, whether or not any mention of this Sacrament is made at all in the New Testament.

It is by the same dart that Luther expects to wound all the rest of the Sacraments.

Against this dart, I will take the same buckler or shield that Luther himself confesses to be impenetrable.

His own words are these: *'truly the Church has this faculty, that it can discern the Word of God, from the word of men,'* even as St. Augustine confesses, that *'he has believed the Gospel by the motion of the Church's authority; which asserts that it was the Gospel.'*

---

sacrament enables the ordained to exercise a sacred power in the name and with the authority of Christ for the service of the People of God (*Compendium*, Number 323).

Therefore, seeing that the Church, as Luther confesses, *'can discern the Word of God from the word of men'*, it is certain that She has that power from none other than God.

And She has it for no other reason than that She may not err in those things that should contain no error.

Out of this foundation that Luther has laid for us, it then follows that the Church has received from God not only the power of discerning God's Word from that of men - which he admits - but also the faculty of discerning between divine and human sense of Scripture. [96]

Otherwise, what is the use for the Church to know by God's teaching the true Scripture from the false one, if She could not distinguish between the false and true sense of true Scripture?

Finally, by the same reason, it follows that God instructs His Church even in things which are not written, lest She might, through errors, embrace false things for true ones.

It would be dangerous if She admitted the writings of men as if they were the words of God, or drew a false sense out of the Word of God, especially if She were to take false Sacraments for true ones and human traditions for divine.

Nay, not only the traditions of men, but it would be more dangerous to accept the inventions of the devil, if the Church of Christ were to place her hope in feigned and vain signs of corporal things, as enchanters do.

It appears, therefore, by Luther's confessing the Church to have the power to discern between the words of God from the words of men, that She has no less power to discern between divine institutions and the traditions of men.

Otherwise, the error which we are to avoid might as well arise from the one side as from the other.

Christ's care for His Church is not that She may not err in this or that manner, but that She may not err in any manner whatsoever.

The greatest error and injury to Christ that the Church could commit would be to put Her trust - which She ought to have in Him alone - in

---

[96] Since they are authentic witnesses of the apostolic faith and are invested with the authority of Christ, the bishops in union with the Pope have the duty of proclaiming the Gospel faithfully and authoritatively to all. By means of a supernatural sense of faith, the people of God unfailingly adhere to the faith under the guidance of the living Magisterium of the Church (*Compendium*, Number 184).

signs not supported by any grace, empty and void of all the advantages of Faith.

Therefore, the Church cannot err about the Sacraments of Faith, no more, I say, than in admitting Scripture, in which Luther confesses her to be infallible. [97]

Otherwise, many absurdities should follow, especially one such as this, that in matters of Faith almost all the teachings the Church has established these many ages past, might be disputed according to the fancy of every new-fangled heretic, which is the most ridiculous thing imaginable.

Luther says that nothing is to be believed with certainty except what is confirmed by Scripture, and clear testimonies of Scripture at that.

Accordingly, we must not assert the perpetual Virginity of the Blessed Virgin Mary.

Moreover, an unexhausted material will be provided for battering the Church at the pleasure of every one who is minded to stir up new sects, or renew the old ones.

For, at any time, there have been few or no heretics who did not pretend to call upon Scripture, everyone arguing their new-broached opinions to be confirmed by Scripture.

They also disputed whether each other's opinions were agreeable to Scripture or not, because the contrary was not defined therein, and that what was alleged against their sects was to be understood otherwise than as the orthodox Church understood it.

And then, lest the truth might be clearly brought against them, they either forged another sense, or preferred some other passages of Scripture, which seemed contrary to the former; struggling in such manner as to make them seem ambiguous.

If the public Faith of the Church had not withstood Arius the heretic, I do not know if he should have ever needed a subject of dispute from Scripture. [98]

---

[97] Infallibility is exercised when the Roman Pontiff, in virtue of his office as the Supreme Pastor of the Church, or the College of Bishops, in union with the Pope especially when joined together in an Ecumenical Council, proclaim by a definitive act a doctrine pertaining to faith or morals. Infallibility is also exercised when the Pope and Bishops in their ordinary Magisterium are in agreement in proposing a doctrine as definitive. Every one of the faithful must adhere to such teaching with the obedience of faith (*Compendium*, Number 185).

[98] The laity participates in the prophetic office by welcoming evermore in faith the Word of Christ and proclaiming it to the world by the witness of their lives, their

Now that we have proved by Luther's own fundamentals that the Sacraments of the Church could not have been instituted except by God Himself, though nothing were read about it in Scripture, let us see whether Scripture makes any mention of this Sacrament.

All men do unanimously confess - Luther alone excepted - that the Apostles were ordained priests by our Saviour at His Last Supper.

There it plainly appears that power was given to them to consecrate the Body of Christ, a power which the Priest alone possesses. [99]

'But, says Luther, *'it is not a Sacrament, because there is no grace promised therein.'*

But pray, how, or whence has he secured this knowledge? *'Because* (says he) *it is not read in Scripture!'*

This is his usual consequence: *'It is not written in the Gospels, therefore it has not been done by Christ'.*

Now, the Evangelist himself overthrows this way of reasoning when he says, *'Many things were done which are not written in this book'* (John 22:25).

But let us touch Luther yet a little closer:

He confesses that the Eucharist is a Sacrament - and he would be mad, if he did not.

But where, pray, does he find in Scripture that grace is promised in that Sacrament?

Since he admits nothing but Scripture and clear Scripture at that, let him read the passages that treat of Our Lord's Supper, and see if he can find in any of the Gospels that grace is promised in the receiving of the Blessed Sacrament.

We read that Christ said, *'this is My Blood of the New Testament, which shall be shed for many unto remission of sins'* (Mt 26:28), whereby He signified, that He should redeem mankind by His Passion upon the Cross.

---

words, their evangelizing action, and by catechesis. This evangelizing action acquires a particular efficacy because it is accomplished in the ordinary circumstances of the world (*Compendium*, Number 190).

[99] The lay faithful participate in the priestly office of Christ especially in the Eucharist by offering as a spiritual sacrifice *"acceptable to God through Jesus Christ"* (1 Peter 2:5) their own lives with all of their works, their prayers, their apostolic undertakings, their family life, their daily work and hardships borne with patience and even their consolations of spirit and body. In this way, even the laity, dedicated to Christ and consecrated by the Holy Spirit, offer to God the world itself (Compendium, Number 189).

But when He said, *'this do for the commemoration of Me'* (1 Cor 11:24), He promised no grace, nor remission of sins to him that does this - that is, to the consecrated priests, or to him that receives the Eucharist.

Nor does the Apostle, in his Epistle to the Corinthians, when he threatens judgment to them that receive the Eucharist unworthily, make mention of any grace to him that receives it worthily.

If anything, the sixth chapter of St. John's Gospel promises Grace to him that receives the Sacrament of our Lord's Body and Blood; still, that makes nothing for Luther, because he denies the whole chapter to have any reference at all to the Eucharist.

You see here, very plainly, that in his whole work he cannot maintain that promise of grace - which he so fairly promised us - as the sole basis of the Sacrament, and only in that Sacrament which he admits.

This is so unless, in addition to the words of Scripture, he has recourse to the Faith of the Church, as it is necessary for him.

Therefore, as it is sufficient for us to read in the Gospel that the power of consecrating the Sacrament was given to those whom the priests succeed, so is it likewise enough that we read the counsel of the Apostle to Timothy, that he should not impose hands rashly upon anyone.

This passage plainly demonstrates that the ordination of priests is not performed by the consent of the laity, as Luther alone affirms.

Instead, it is by the ordination of a Bishop only, and that by a certain imposition of hands, in which God, through the exterior sign, infuses an interior grace. [100]

Now concerning this grace, why shouldn't we believe the Church of the Living God, since She is *'the Pillar and Ground of the Truth'*, as the Apostle says (1 Tim 3:15)?

Luther himself must certainly believe the Church concerning the grace promised in the Eucharist, because it is by the Faith of the Church that the promise of that grace - or the giving of it without any promise - is known.

It amazes me, indeed, that anyone should be so distracted as to doubt whether grace is given by the Sacrament of Orders to the priest of the Gospel.

We read in many places that seem to signify that grace was conferred on the priests of the old Law, and that God says, *'take unto thee also*

---

[100] Only validly ordained bishops, as successors of the apostles, can confer the sacrament of Holy Orders (*Compendium*, Number 332).

Aaron thy brother with his sons, from among the children of Israel, that they may minister to me in the priest's office' (Ex 28:1).

Otherwise, what should this exterior sanctification have signified for the honour of God, if God had not likewise infused grace, by which they should be likewise inwardly sanctified?

And that also through Christ, the faith of Whose coming gave force and strength to previous Sacraments, even as it made the Jews capable of obtaining eternal salvation?

But if anyone will not admit that grace was conferred to the priesthood of the Old Law, he has no reason to deny the infusion of grace into the priests of the Gospel Law, because now the fullness of grace has come through the Passion of Christ. [101]

In the Acts of the Apostles, when St. Paul and Barnabas were set apart for that work to which the Holy Ghost had called them, (Acts 13) they were not sent away before they were first ordained by imposition of hands.

But, pray, why did the Apostles lay hands on them? [102]

Was it to touch their bodies in a vain manner, without profiting their souls by spiritual grace?

Considering that this Sacrament was used by the Apostles, how then Luther dare affirm that it was unknown to the Church of Christ?

'But it was never called a Sacrament by any of the ancient Doctors, (says he) *except Dyonisius, because we read nothing at all of these Sacraments in the other Fathers, neither did they think on the name of Sacrament, whenever they spoke of these things; because the invention of Sacraments is new'.*

An *excellent* reason of Luther's, I must confess, yet altogether false.

---

[101] This sacrament was prefigured in the Old Covenant in the service of the Levites, in the priesthood of Aaron, and in the institution of the seventy "Elders" (Numbers 11:25). These prefigurations find their fulfillment in Christ Jesus who by the sacrifice of the cross is the "one mediator between God and man" (1 Timothy 2:5), the *"High Priest according to the order of Melchizedek"* (Hebrews 5:10). The one priesthood of Christ is made present in the ministerial priesthood (*Compendium*, Number 324).

[102] The sacrament of Holy Orders is conferred, in each of its three degrees, by means of the imposition of hands on the head of the ordinand by the Bishop who pronounces the solemn prayer of consecration. With this prayer he asks God on behalf of the ordinand for the special outpouring of the Holy Spirit and for the gifts of the Spirit proper to the ministry to which he is being ordained (*Compendium*, Number 331).

And, if it was true, still it could avail nothing for his purpose.

If the Ancients had not written at all about something, it is perhaps because it was never disputed amongst them.

Or because when they did write of it, they signified it by its proper name and not by that common name of Sacrament.

Should it then follow, as a necessary consequence, that there has been no Order at all, or that it was not a Sacrament?

If anybody should call Baptism by the proper name of Baptism, and should not add the word Sacrament, shall it be said, therefore, that he does not think Baptism to be a Sacrament?

Moreover, even if it was Dyonisius alone, amongst all the holy Fathers, who wrote that Orders is a Sacrament; that by itself should be sufficient to destroy Luther's objection, whereby he intends to make people believe that the invention of Sacraments is new!

Luther contradicts this novelty by confessing that it was written by Dyonisius, whom he acknowledges to be ancient.

And this would be true, if St. Dyonisius were as sacrilegious a man as Luther pretends him to be, when he says that *'he* (Dyonisius) *had almost no solid learning in him; that none of the things he wrote in his Ecclesiastical Hierarchy are proved by authority or reason.*

'They are all his own inventions, and much like dreams; he is pernicious in his Mystical Divinity, which some ignorant divines (says Luther*) extol so much; more like a Platonist than a Christian; in which you will not learn who Christ is, and, if you had known Him before, you should lose your belief in Him.*

'I speak (says he) *by experience'* - by the experience, I suppose, of losing Christ himself.

And further; *'pray, what does he perform in his Ecclesiastical Hierarchy, but only allegorically describes some ecclesiastical rites?'*

Finally, that he might show in how light a matter St. Dyonisius lost his labour, Luther says, *'do you think it should be difficult for me to sport with allegories in whatsoever is credited? It should not be any hard work for me to write a better Hierarchy than that of Dyonisius.'*

Who can patiently endure to see the pious labours of the holy man Dyonisius so much abused by this jangler, as if he were raging against some heretic like himself?

Luther calls Dyonisius illiterate and foolish, and one who writes not only dreams, but also pernicious doctrines, destroying Christ!

All these reproaches are, notwithstanding, to the glory of the holy man, whose works are all sufficiently demonstrated to be good, by their displeasing a man as wicked as Luther.

For what agreement can there be between light and darkness, between Christ and Belial?

Luther's own wicked brain was the reason that he gained no good by the pious books of this holy man.

Horatius wrote truthfully, *'unless the vessel is sweet, whatsoever you put therein will become sour.'*

In as much as Luther says that he, *'could write a better Hierarchy than that of St. Dyonisius'*, pray let him brag of it when he has done it.

In the meanwhile, he undertakes something much more difficult when he goes about to demolish that Hierarchy which is founded upon a solid rock.

The indignation I have conceived at that impious fellow's casting of such injurious reproaches against the holy man has caused me to digress somewhat.

But, as I began to say, if St. Dyonisius had been the man who taught holy Orders to be a Sacrament, this alone would be sufficient to convince Luther when he asserts that the invention of the Sacraments is a new thing.

Luther does not only confess Dyonisius to be ancient, but also that all the Christian world honours him as a Saint.

Thus, Luther's anger against him is caused merely by malice, which doesn't permit him to tolerate anything contrary to his wicked heresies.

In order that his vanity the more plainly appear everywhere, I will show that not only St. Dyonisius but also St. Gregory and St. Augustine - whom Luther falsely calls his Patron - believe Orders to be a Sacrament.

Luther derides the indelible character of the Sacrament, although not calling it by that name. However, St. Jerome writes clearly enough about the character of the Sacrament of Baptism, and St. Augustine teaches the same on both the Sacraments of Baptism and Orders. [103]

---

[103] The sacramental character is a spiritual "seal" bestowed by the sacraments of Baptism, Confirmation, and Holy Orders. It is a promise and guarantee of divine protection. By virtue of this seal the Christian is configured to Christ, participates in a variety of ways in his priesthood and takes his part in the Church according to different states and functions. He is, therefore, set apart for divine worship and the service of the Church. Because this character is indelible the sacraments that impress it on the soul are received only once in life (*Compendium*, Number 227).

On the character of Baptism, I will begin with St. Jerome so that the character of Orders may appear more evidently.

Regarding its indelibility, both St. Augustine and St. Gregory compare it with the Sacrament of Orders.

St. Jerome, therefore, on these words of St. Paul to the Ephesians, *'grieve not the Holy Spirit of God: whereby you are sealed unto the day of redemption'* (Eph 4:30), writes thus:

'But we have been signed with the Holy Ghost that our spirit and soul may be sealed with the signet of God, and that we may receive that image and likeness after which we were first created.

'This seal of the Holy Ghost, according to the words of our Saviour, is stamped by God Himself. Because, he says, this has God the Father sealed' (John 6:27).

And a little after, *'he is therefore signed that he may keep the seal, and that he may, in the Day of Redemption, show it pure, sincere, and unchanged; that therefore he may receive his reward with those who are redeemed.'*

Among all those who have written on the character of Sacraments, no one could have more plainly expressed the character - whereby God Almighty signs the soul through the Sacraments - than St. Jerome has done.

He has not done so by human fiction - as Luther, that execrable scoffer of Sacraments, feigns - but rather by solid testimonies of Holy Scriptures.

A character is that quality of the soul which God Almighty - by reasons best known to Himself, and inscrutable to us - impresses as a seal to identify His own flock from strangers.

But this character can never be erased, though they stain it with vices and turn it from white to black, from perfect to imperfect, from most pure to impure.

In the Day of Judgment, those signed with it will be known to the entire world, to be of His flock, marked by Him with that signet. [104]

This is the only reason why the Church so constantly observes the renewal of the other Sacraments – i.e., the Eucharist, Penance, Marriage, Extreme Unction – but not Baptism, Confirmation and Holy Orders.

---

[104] This sacrament yields a special outpouring of the Holy Spirit which configures the recipient to Christ in his triple office as Priest, Prophet, and King, according to the respective degrees of the sacrament. Ordination confers an indelible spiritual character and therefore cannot be repeated or conferred for a limited time (*Compendium*, Number 335).

She has learned from the Holy Ghost that the seal of the character is imprinted in these Sacraments so that it cannot be defaced, therefore ought not to be repeated.

To show more evidently that Orders are, in this case, similar to Baptism, let us hear St. Gregory:

'It is ridiculous to say that he who has received Holy Orders ought to receive them again; because, as he who has once been baptised, ought not to be baptised again; so he, who has been once consecrated, ought not to be consecrated again in the same degree of Orders.'

You see that the Church does not permit the Sacrament of Orders to be repeated any more than that of Baptism, by reason of its indelible character.

But to shut Luther's mouth, who calls that character *'a feigned thing and that St. Dyonisius was the only man of all the ancient Fathers that called Holy Orders a Sacrament'*, we will, as we have promised, give you St. Augustine's words.

Addressing Baptism and Holy Orders, he speaks thus:

'They are both Sacraments, and given to man after certain consecration, the one at his Baptism, the other when he receives Holy Orders. Therefore, it is not lawful in the Holy Catholic Church to repeat either of them.

'When any heretical minister is received into the Church and if, after the error of schism is corrected, it should seem necessary, for the good of peace that he should exercise the same office that he had before, yet he is not to be ordained again.

'As Baptism remains entire in them, so Orders also. The sin consisted in the schism, not in the Sacraments, which are the same wherever they are.'

And later he writes, *'injury must be done to neither of the two Sacraments.'*

And on the Sacrament of Orders he adds that *'as he that breaks off from unity, has it not rightly, yet has it; so likewise he does not rightly give it, yet gives it.'*

And returning again to both: *'the Sacraments of Christ and His Church are not hindered if heretics and wicked persons use them unlawfully; these men are to be corrected and punished, but the Sacraments acknowledged and venerated.'*

Thus, you see that what Luther boasts so boldly is void of Truth: *'the Sacrament of Holy Orders was unknown to the Church of Christ: the character is an idle fiction; the invention of Sacrament is a new thing; Holy Orders were no Sacrament among the ancients'.*

Luther cannot separate such persons from the Church of Christ - for they were illustrious in Her by Doctrine of Faith and exemplary lives. You see that everything Luther has said has been rejected by their testimony.

He cannot reckon them among the moderns either, unless a thousand years be with him as one day (Ps 89:4).

Notwithstanding this, he opposes all the reasons, authority, and faith of all by this one argument:

'We are all priests' (says Luther) according to that passage of St. Peter, *'you are a kingly priesthood'* (1 Pet 2:9), but as one cannot be more a man than another, so one can be no more a priest than another.

'Those, therefore, who are called priests, are none other than laymen, chosen only by the consent of the people, or elected by the Bishop, not without the people.

'Because to preach and ordain are nothing but mere ministry without anything of Sacrament'.

We have not only faithfully repeated his argument, but also freely set down whatever may support him.

And yet who would not laugh at this doltish divine?

If the Order of Priesthood is therefore nothing because every Christian is a priest, then by the same reason it must follow that Christ was no greater than Saul.

David said of Saul, *peccavi tangens Christum Domini*: I have sinned in touching the Anointed (Christum) of our Lord; or that Christ had nothing above them, of Whom it is said, *'nolite tangere Christos meos,'* touch not Mine anointed.

Finally, that God had nothing above all those of whom He said by the Prophet, *'I have said ye are gods, and are all the Sons of the Most High'*.

In summation, Luther contends that all Christians are kings in the same manner that they are priests: For it is not only said, *'ye are a royal Priesthood'*, but also *'a priestly kingdom'*.

Let us diligently observe what this serpent intends, who, I suppose, is too crafty to think that this argument is of any consequence.

He only licks that he may bite afterwards.

He extols the laity to the priesthood for only one reason, that he may reduce priests to the rank of the laity, denying Priesthood to be a Sacrament, and making it a mere custom of electing a preacher.

And he says that *'he who preaches is no more a priest than the other; nay, no more a priest than a painted man is a man'*.

He is opposes St. Paul, who, writing to Timothy, says, *'let the priests that rule well be esteemed worthy of double honour, especially they who labour in the Word and Doctrine'* (1 Tim 5:17).

By this, the Apostle evidently teaches that although those priests who labour in the Word and Doctrine are most worthy of double honour, yet those who do not so labour, but only govern well, are also priests and merit double honour. [105]

Otherwise, he would not have said, *'especially those who labour in the Word and Doctrine'*, but only such as labour therein.

Furthermore, so that Luther may not be able to maintain what he says, that is, *'that the Priest's office is nothing but to preach to the people: for to say Mass is nothing but to receive Communion for himself'*, I say: let us again hear the Apostle's words to prove the falsehood of Luther's statement:

'For every high priest taken from among men is ordained for men in the things that appertain to God, that he may offer up gifts and sacrifices for sins' (Heb 5:1).

Does not this plainly show us that a priest's duty requires from him to offer sacrifices to God for men?

Although writing to the Hebrews, he did not suggest that Christians should become Jewish, even though he clearly spoke of the Priesthood of both Laws.

Thus, Luther is twice pressed by this testimony, because the Apostle also teaches that the Mass is a sacrifice and to be offered for the people.

Seeing that the Church offers no other sacrifice, he teaches that the duty of offering is the chief part of the priest's charge, and that no one but a priest can consecrate our Lord's Body.

And, indeed, if Luther's words were true, you may easily see what follows: that thousands of priests without the gift of preaching are not truly priests - but only equivocally called priests, just as a painted man is called a man.

---

[105] The anointing of the Spirit seals the priest with an indelible, spiritual character that configures him to Christ the priest and enables him to act in the name of Christ the Head. As a co-worker of the order of bishops he is consecrated to preach the Gospel, to celebrate divine worship, especially the Eucharist from which his ministry draws its strength, and to be a shepherd of the faithful (*Compendium*, Number 328).

That would mean that almost all the Christian world has no other God or people but idolaters, adoring bread for Christ, and bending their knees to Baal.

Regarding the right of electing, as he calls it, he attributes that power to the people.

In one place he seems to give this rite indifferently to the Bishop and people, when he says that, *'although it is certain all Christians are equally priests, and they have a like power in all the Sacraments: yet none can lawfully exercise this power, without the consent of the congregation or the vocation of a superior.'*

Yet, in another place, he gives the greatest right to the people.

Speaking of priests, he says:

'If they were compelled to admit all of us who have been baptised equally to be priests, as indeed we are; and that the ministry is only given to them by our consent; then they should know also that they have no right of ruling over us, except what we permit them of our own free will.'

Now once these two places are compared together, it shows his opinion to be that *'the people, without the Bishop can ordain priests; but not the Bishop without the people,'* as it appears by his saying that *'the ministry only is permitted to the priests and that not without the consent of the people.'*

Now if this is true, a priest cannot be ordained without the people's consent.

Thus, *'it is only by their consent -* says he *- that Bishops were formerly made rulers of the Church.*

'It cannot be denied - says Luther *- that the true Churches were formerly governed by Elders, without the ordinations and consecrations; being chosen to this, by reason of their age and long experience in things of that kind.'*

Pray, let him show us where he finds these things?

For my part, I believe they are false. [106]

If every layman has equal power over any of the Sacraments as a priest; and if the Order of Priesthood stands for nothing, why does the

---

[106] Ordained priests in the exercise of their sacred ministry speak and act not on their own authority, nor even by mandate or delegation of the community, but rather in the Person of Christ the Head and in the name of the Church. Therefore, the ministerial priesthood differs essentially and not just in degree from the priesthood common to all the faithful for whose service Christ instituted it (*Compendium*, Number 336).

Apostle write thus to Timothy, *'neglect not the grace that is in thee, which was given thee by prophecy, with imposition of the hands of the priesthood'* (1 Tim 4:14)?

And in another place, he writes, *'I admonish thee that thou stir up the grace of God which is in thee by the imposition of my hands'* (2 Tim 1:6).

Again, *'impose not hands lightly upon any man, neither be partaker of other men's sins'* (1 Tim 5:22).

Finally, these are the words of the Apostle to Titus: *'for this cause I left thee in Crete: that thou shouldest set in order the things that are wanting and shouldest ordain priests in every city, as I also appointed thee'* (Tit 1:5).

Now, reader, that you have seen in a few words some passages of the Apostle, you may, by comparison, easily discover that whatsoever Luther has vented in such a disorderly fashion against Order are mere fictions and lies.

For what he says that *'is done by the people's consent,'* St. Paul shows to be done by the Bishop, while he says that he has left him (Titus) at Crete to the end that he should ordain priests in the cities, not rashly, but as the Apostle himself had appointed when present.

You see, by this, that priests are ordained by imposition of the hands.

And, so that no one may doubt that grace is also given at the same time, you see that it is conferred by imposition of hands: *'stir up the grace of God which is in thee by the imposition of my hands'* (2 Tim 1:6).

And this also, *'neglect not the grace that is in thee, which was given thee by prophecy, with imposition of the hands of the priesthood'* (1 Tim 4:14).

Take notice of these things.

I am amazed that Luther is not ashamed to deny the Sacrament of Holy Orders, as he is not ignorant that the words of St. Paul are in every man's hands.

The Apostle's words teach that a priest cannot be ordained except by a Bishop, and not without consecration in which both the visible sign is put on and much spiritual grace infused, that he who is consecrated not only receives the Holy Ghost for himself, but also the power of imparting Him to others.

Can it be that what the Apostle has written is new, just because Luther said so?

How can those words be unknown to the Church, since they are and have been read at all times throughout the universal Church of Christ?

By these things, it is clear that what Luther has railed out so confidently against Holy Orders, not one syllable is true, but mere lying inventions of his malice.

Chapter XIII

Of the Sacrament of Extreme Unction

 N THIS SACRAMENT of Extreme Unction, Luther scoffs at the Church twice in order that he himself may be derided twice. Firstly, he says that *'Divines do call this unction a Sacrament'*, as if *'Divines'* – as he calls them - were the only men who called it a Sacrament.

Secondly, he scoffs at their calling it *'Extreme'*.

And Luther, in a joking manner, objects to what he can never answer in earnest: for it may be rightly called Extreme, as being the last of four.

Afterwards, to show that it is not a Sacrament, Luther first objects to what he foresees everybody will object against him, that is, the words of St. James the Apostle:

'Is any man sick among you? Let him bring in the priests of the church and let them pray over him, anointing him with oil in the name of the Lord. And the prayer of faith shall save the sick man. And the Lord shall raise him up: and if he be in sins, they shall be forgiven him' (Jas 5:14-15).

According to his own definition, these words evidently testify that Extreme Unction is a Sacrament, having both a visible sign and a promise of grace. [107]

However, Luther immediately and most impudently begins to deride these words, as if they were of no importance:

'For my part, (says he) *I say that if ever there was folly acted, it is especially in this place.'*

And I, again on the contrary, do affirm that if Luther was ever mad at any time - as indeed his madness appears almost in every place - he is certainly troubled here, in the Sacrament of Extreme Unction, to an extreme height of madness.

'I omit (says he) *saying that many do probably assert this not to be the Epistle of the Apostle St. James, nor worthy of an apostolic spirit, though by custom, whosoever it be, it has obtained authority.*

'Yet if it were certainly written by the Apostle St. James, I should say that it is not lawful for an Apostle to institute a Sacrament by his own authority; that is, to give a divine promise, with a sign joined thereunto. This belongs to Christ alone.

'St. Paul says that he received from our Lord the Sacrament of the Eucharist, and that he was sent, not to baptise, but rather to preach the Gospel: But nowhere in the Gospel do we read of the Sacrament of Extreme Unction.'

---

[107] Having received from the Lord the charge to heal the sick, the Church strives to carry it out by taking care of the sick and accompanying them with her prayer of intercession. Above all, the Church possesses a sacrament specifically intended for the benefit of the sick. This sacrament was instituted by Christ and is attested by Saint James: *"Is anyone among you sick? Let him call in the presbyters of the Church and let them pray over him and anoint him with oil in the name of the Lord"* (James 5:14-15) – (*Compendium*, Number 315).

You see how he endeavours here, in two ways, to weaken the words of the Apostle:

First, he questions the Epistle having been written by the Apostle.

Secondly, even if it were written by him, he denies the Apostle's authority of instituting Sacraments.

Although he has proposed these two things in a few words, he passes hastily onto some other. Yet they are the chief weapons by which he intends to destroy this Sacrament.

Whatever else he says is trivial, taking occasion to laugh, as if the Church did not do well in keeping this Sacrament.

But these two things amount to one: if the Epistle had not been written by the Apostle, or was not worthy of an apostolic spirit, or if the Apostle gave this unction as a Sacrament it would not be more approved to be one. Nevertheless, it should plainly follow that these words of Luther amount to nothing.

If he had said that others before him doubted whose Epistle this was, he would have told the truth.

The Church admits nothing rashly. She discusses everything diligently, so that everything She receives may be believed with greater certitude, even though directed only by human concurrence.

But he says that *'many do assert this Epistle, not only not to be of the Apostle's writing, but also unworthy of an apostolic spirit'*; and that *'they not only assert, but probably assert this.'*

It is more than probable that he cannot prove what he says.

Otherwise, let him name some of these many persons, who, if they are members of the Church, I suppose they are neither so many in number nor of so great authority, as to be able to stand out against the whole Church.

But so far he has produced none.

I will therefore cite one who may suffice against his many, namely, St. Jerome, who, in Holy Scriptures, was the most learned of his time, and has distinguished himself as one able discern between dubious and real things.

This great man had for some time remained doubtful about the Epistle of St. Paul, but only before such time when a full consent of the whole Church had not yet confirmed it. He pronounced the Epistle of St. James to be undoubtedly of his own writing.

His words are these: *'St. James, St. Peter, St. Jude, and St. John have published seven Epistles, as mystical as they are succinct and short; yea, likewise long; short in words, and long in sentences, so that there are not many who would not be blinded by reading them.'*

The same St. Jerome speaks thus of the seven canonical Epistles:

'The first of them is one of St. James', the second, of St. Peter's, three of St. John's, and one of St. Jude's.'

You see how this Father has the same opinion of St. James' Epistle that he has of St. Peter's. Nor does he think it unworthy of an apostolic spirit.

Truly, if Luther had given us any reasons why this Epistle should not be accounted as St. James' - as if written by some other person, who spoke in the same manner - he would be more tolerable somehow.

But now he says, *'it is improbable that it should be St. James, because it is unworthy of an apostolic spirit.'*

In this regard, I will bring no objections against Luther but Luther's own, because no one has ever contradicted Luther more frequently and strongly than Luther himself.

In the Sacrament of Holy Orders, he says, *'the Church has power given her to discern the Word of God from the words of men.'*

How, then, can he say that this Epistle is unworthy of an apostolic spirit, since the Church, whose judgment cannot err in this - as he himself confesses - has judged it to be full of apostolic spirit?

Therefore, he has now, by his own wisdom, so hemmed himself in on all sides that he must necessarily consent that either this Epistle belongs to the Apostle - contrary to what he has affirmed to be probable - or that the Church can err in distinguishing Scripture, which he previously denied.

If he says that the Church has approved as worthy of an apostolic spirit what is unworthy, then he is a blasphemer against the Church.

If he holds that the Apostle has written what is unworthy of an Apostle, then is he a blasphemer against the Apostle.

We have, therefore, sufficiently confuted this.

Indeed, he has sufficiently confuted himself, in denying the Epistle to belong to the Apostle, or to be worthy of an apostolic spirit.

Now we come to a point at which, like a valiant man, he openly attacks the Apostle himself, saying: *'although it was of the Apostle's writing, yet it is not lawful for an Apostle to institute a Sacrament by his own authority. That is, to give a divine promise with a sign adjoined to it: for this* (says he) *belongs to Christ alone.'*

O this *happy age*, in which Luther, this new *Doctor of the Gentiles*, is risen! He who, by resisting an Apostle to his face for not going the right way to the Gospel of Christ, will appear to follow the example of St. Paul (Gal 2:11-14).

On the contrary – he can be accused of more than teaching Gentiles to become Judaizers – for he has arrogated to himself the power of promising grace and instituting Sacraments.

Here Luther accuses the Apostle of usurping the power of Christ, like the proud and traitorous Angel, who said, *'I will ascend into heaven, I will exalt my throne above the stars of God, I will sit in the mountain of the covenant, in the sides of the north'* (Is 14:13-14).

The Pope has no great reason to be distressed at Luther's reproaches, he who charges such enormous crimes upon the Apostle himself.

Since it is certain that this Epistle belongs to the Apostle, what else does Luther do but manifestly accuse the Apostle of having instituted this Sacrament without authority and against all right?

Nay, even if he denies that the Epistle belongs to the Apostle – thereby excusing himself from his calumny - he professes that, if it were of the Apostle's own writing, he would say just as much!

Indeed, some think that the Apostle received power of instituting Sacraments with the power of the Holy Ghost, which God sent them at Pentecost, and of which Christ had foretold, *'the Paraclete, the Holy Ghost, Whom the Father will send in My Name, He will teach you all things and bring all things to your mind whatsoever I shall have said to you.'* (John 14:26).

Yet at this time I shall not dispute whether or not an Apostle has such power, because it is not necessary to dispute it now.

I do not doubt that this unction is really a Sacrament, since it is evident that the Apostle gives it to us as a Sacrament.

But I doubt that the Apostle was so impiously arrogant as to give the people something as a Sacrament, which, in reality, was not.

If the Apostle himself did not have the power to institute this Sacrament, then he delivered it to the people in the words he received from Christ.

Christ revealed some things to the world by St. Matthew, some by St. Luke, some by St. John, and some by the Apostle St. Paul. Why is it not possible that He should be pleased to make known some things unto us by the Apostle St. James?

Luther, having thus strenuously opposed the Apostle, begins now to turn himself against the Church altogether.

He says that She 'abuses the words of the Apostle, in not administering this unction to the sick, but when at the point of death:' whereas St. James says, 'if any be sick, not if any be dying.'

As if in every light fever - contracted, perhaps, by too much drinking - the Church sinned in not giving so great a thing as a Sacrament freely and without restraint; or, in not attributing to herself a miracle in healing such disease, as either sleep or abstinence can cure.

So that there may be no room for doubt, the Apostle writes sick, and yet did not mean a man in every light sickness, but one troubled with such sickness as may show to be taken away by virtue of the Sacrament, if he is cured. [108]

Also, that this Sacrament is not to be administered except in great sickness and by all the prayers which are said over the sick person. Such prayers are, no doubt, very ancient, and not of the new invention of those whom Luther calls *Divines*.

Although they do not promise an assured health of the body, yet they do not despair of health.

Nor do they (as Luther says) come only to those who are undoubtedly sure to die; because, if they were sure of his death, it would be in vain to pray for his health.

Therefore, the Church's intention is not - as he impertinently cavils - that this should be the last Sacrament, although it is so called.

On the contrary, it is so that the sick person may recover his health, which, even if God is not pleased that he should, it is no prejudice to the force and virtue of the Sacrament, which tends more to the curing of the soul than to the health of the body. [109]

---

[108] This sacrament confers a special grace which unites the sick person more intimately to the Passion of Christ for his good and for the good of all the Church. It gives comfort, peace, courage, and even the forgiveness of sins if the sick person is not able to make a confession. Sometimes, if it is the will of God, this sacrament even brings about the restoration of physical health. In any case this Anointing prepares the sick person for the journey to the Father's House (*Compendium*, Number 319).

[109] Any member of the faithful can receive this sacrament as soon as he or she begins to be in danger of death because of sickness or old age. The faithful who receive this sacrament can receive it several times if their illness becomes worse or another serious sickness afflicts them. The celebration of this sacrament should, if possible, be preceded by individual confession on the part of the sick person (*Compendium*, Number 316).

Concerning the efficacy of the sign, Luther's reason is altogether without reason or efficacy:

'If that unction be a Sacrament (says he), *it ought without doubt, to be an effectual sign of what it promises; but it promises the health and recovery of the sick, as appears by the words, 'the prayers of the faithful shall save the sick, and our Lord will raise him up'.*

'Yet who does not see but this promise is fulfilled in very few? What shall we say then? (says he), *for either the Apostle speaks falsely in this promise, or else this unction is no Sacrament. Because a sacramental promise is certain, but this, for the most part, fails.'*

It appears by this only argument that Luther does not care much about how open his calumnies are, so that he can, under some pretext of truth, impose upon the unwary.

He is not ashamed to object against the Divines, attributing to them what they have never said.

'A Sacrament (says he) *is, according to their sayings, an effectual sign of what it promises; but this Sacrament does not give the health of the body, which it promises.'*

But the Divines say no such thing.

They say it is an effectual sign of grace, defining it thus: *'a Sacrament is a visible sign of invisible grace.'*

They do not speak of the health of the body, which may be given without grace.

So when he says that *'if unction is a Sacrament, the Apostle lies,'* it is Luther himself that lies.

The Sacrament, inasmuch as it is a Sacrament, by a corporeal sign promises the health of the soul but not of the body.

Nevertheless, Luther includes not only the Apostle but also Christ Himself under the same lie, if Unction were not a Sacrament.

Because, without the Sacrament, the words and promise ought to be true also.

Therefore, when the Apostle says that the sick shall be healed by unction and prayers, and when Christ says, *'these signs shall follow them that believe in Him:... They shall lay their hand upon the sick: and they shall recover'* (Mk 16:17-18), who does not see that sometimes these things are performed, but not always?

Those who promised them are not lying, either, by whatever words they promised corporeal things; yet, everybody knows they never promised them to be perpetual, since the body - in which they are to be done - cannot last forever.

But here we are to understand that they refer to spiritual things, because the spirit is to live for ever.

Luther's sentence exacts from the Divines that, if Unction is a Sacrament, it must always cure and must not be an ineffectual sign. He undertakes to prove that it cannot be a Sacrament if it does not render the body immortal.

Now this, nevertheless, he himself promises to be done by the prayers of good men, without the least staggering in faith: *'there is no doubt,* (says he) *but at this day, as many as we please may be cured.'*

Now if this is true, a faith such as this may preserve man immortal.

It is probable indeed, seeing that this may be done by a stable and undoubtful faith - not only sometimes, but, as he affirms, always.

I wonder if anyone could ever encounter such a faith.

Without a doubt, Luther is a man of such 'faith'. He has so much of it that, in its favour, he almost bids defiance to good works. He is likewise one to whom God has revealed many and great 'mysteries', and who erects a new 'Church', for which miracles are absolutely necessary.

Therefore, it is likely that Luther can abundantly perform whatever can be done by faith.

If this is true, I wonder if he does not cure every dying person! Daily we look for news from Germany of his raising the dead.

Nevertheless, for all this, we hear that not only is no one cured by him, but that many good and innocent priests are killed by his adherents and cruelly murdered for his sake so that, by his example, he may teach that *'Holy Orders is nothing; character is a fiction. David was timorous for repenting himself to have touched the Lord's anointed'* (1 Kgs 26:11,23).

These are Luther's cures, wrought by his great faith, without good works.

Seeing that he kills and does not cure, it is evident that, *'prayers are to be made not only by Faith, but also by good men',* as he says.

Thus, Luther, not being a good man himself, can therefore cure no one.

'This Unction (says he) *'is no Sacrament, because it does not always heal the Body.'*

But he himself is a *holy man*, by whom - as it is reported - the body is killed, and certainly souls are killed.

Luther claims that St. James writes nothing worthy of an apostolic spirit.

But, of course, Luther writes everything worthy of such a spirit, and discerns things unworthy of it and against the whole Church.

And yet he acknowledges that the Church cannot be deceived in discerning such Scripture.

In this regard, I read St. James' Epistle and saw in it so many things worthy of an apostolic spirit, such as the joy in overcoming temptations; patience in adversity; wisdom to be begged from God; hopes to be placed in God without staggering, and many other such things.

Since all of these are read in the Apostle, I much wonder what reason Luther had to think them unworthy to have been written by an Apostle.

Perhaps Luther wishes that the Apostle had written such things as that *'the Mass is not profitable to the people'*, or that *'Order is a vain fiction,'* and such like, as he himself writes, as things *worthy of an apostolic spirit.*

I am amazed as to why Luther should be so much displeased with St. James's Epistle.

And yet, having read it more attentively, I do not wonder at all.

I find that by his writings, the Apostle touches Luther so narrowly everywhere, as if, by his prophetic spirit, he had plainly foreseen him.

When Luther, under the pretext of faith, despises good works, St. James, on the other hand, disputes, by reason, Scripture and example that 'Faith without works is dead'.

By bitter words, the Apostle resists that prattling petulance of Luther in more than one place:

'If any man think himself to be religious, not bridling his tongue but deceiving his own heart, this man's religion is vain' (Jas 1:26).

Besides, Luther frets at this, which he sees very fitly may be applied to his own tongue: *'the tongue no man can tame, an unquiet evil, full of deadly poison'* (Jas 3:8).

Finally, Luther perceives that what the Apostle has written against contentious persons is truly spoken against his own opinions:

'Who is a wise man and imbued with knowledge, among you? Let him show, by a good conversation, his work in the meekness of wisdom.

'But if you have bitter zeal, and there be contentions in your hearts: glory not and be not liars against the truth. For this is not wisdom, descending from above: but earthly, sensual, devilish.

'For where envying and contention is: there is inconstancy and every evil work.

'But the wisdom that is from above, first indeed is chaste, then peaceable, modest, easy to be persuaded, consenting to the good, full of mercy and good fruits, without judging, without dissimulation.

'And the fruit of justice is sown in peace, to them that make peace' (Jas 3:13-18 ff).

These, gentle Reader, are the words which move Luther to wrath against the Apostle.

These, I say, are the words whereby the Apostle openly touches Luther's petulance, railings, wicked and contentious opinions; even as if he had seen him and read his words.

I do not question that his Epistle, even though so much despised by Luther, will sufficiently prove to all Christians the Sacrament of Extreme Unction.

Nor shall Luther ever be so powerful as to be able to abolish any Sacraments, which have been received by the Church for the salvation of the faithful.

The gates of hell shall never prevail against the Church, much less this single brother, who is but a sooty wicket of hell.

Postface

IN THIS LITTLE BOOK, courteous Reader, I hope I have clearly demonstrated how absurdly and impiously Luther has handled the Holy Sacraments.

Although I have not touched on everything contained in his book, I suppose I have treated more than is even necessary to defend the Sacraments, which was my only design - though not so sufficiently as I might have. Postface

It would not be difficult to enrich this discourse with more plentiful arguments, laws, and sentences of the Holy Fathers, and Scripture itself.

And yet it does not behove me to insist on it any longer, because for Luther such added effort would be vain, and for others what I have written here is more than necessary.

It is as easy for the Ethiopian to change his colour or the leopard his spots as it is for Luther to be converted by teaching.

Even if I had said nothing at all, I do not doubt that there are very learned men everywhere who have uncovered this matter much more clearly than I, in order that others may understand how false and wicked Luther's doctrine is - lest they be so far deceived as to have a good opinion of him.

If anyone desires to be familiar with this strange work of Luther, I think I have made it sufficiently clear to them.

From the foregoing, it is evident to all men what sacrilegious opinions he has of the Sacrament of Our Lord's Body, from which the sanctity of all the other Sacraments flows.

If I had said nothing else, who would have doubted how unworthily and without scruple he treats all the rest of the Sacraments?

As you have seen, he has handled them in such a manner that he abolishes and destroys them all, except Baptism.

That too, he has abused and deprived of all grace, leaving it for no other end than an insolent treatment of penance.

In some Sacraments, he denies the sign; in others, the matter itself.

He neither proves anything in such a great matter, nor presents anything in confirmation of his doctrine.

He contents himself only in denying whatever the Church admits.

By his vain reason he alone laughs at what everybody believes, claiming that he admits nothing except by clear and evident Scriptures.

And, if anyone alleges the Scriptures to be against him, he either evades them by some private exposition of his own, or else denies them to belong to their own authors.

None of the Doctors are so ancient, none so holy, none of so great authority in treating of Holy Scripture than this new doctor, this *little saint*, this *man of learning* rejects with such great authority.

Seeing therefore that he despises all men and believes none, he ought not to object if everybody discredits him again.

I am so far from intending to hold any further dispute with him that I almost repent myself of what I have already argued against him.

For what is gained by disputing against a man who disagrees with everyone, even with himself?

What he affirms in one place he denies in another, denying what he presently affirms.

If you object by faith, he combats by reason; if you touch him with reason, he pretends faith; if you allege philosophers, he flies to Scripture; if you propound Scripture, he trifles with sophistry.

He is ashamed of nothing, fears none, and thinks himself under no law; he contemns the ancient Doctors of the Church, derides the new ones in the highest degree and loads with reproaches the Head Bishop of the Church.

Finally, he undervalues the customs, doctrine, manners, laws, decrees and faith of the Church so much - yea, the whole Church itself - that he almost denies there is any such thing as a Church, except perhaps such a one as he himself makes up of two or three heretics, of whom he himself is chief.

Therefore, he has no solid or certain principle between himself and his adversary.

He requires to be free, lawfully to assert or deny whatever pleases him and as often as it pleases him.

Neither reason, Scripture, custom, laws, human nor does divine authority bind him.

Thus, I thought it unfit to dispute with him any longer, nor to contend by painful reason against his heresies, which he confirms by no reason.

I rather advise all Christians to shun Luther as the most exterminating of plagues, as he who endeavours to bring into the Church of Christ such foul prodigies - the very doctrine of Antichrist.

If one who plans to carry out a schism is to be uprooted with all care, with what great efforts is one to be rooted out who, not only sows dissention but stirs up the people against the Pope, children against their parents, Christians against the Vicar of Christ?

Finally, Luther endeavours to dissolve the whole Church of Christ by his tumults, brawls and contentions; the Church which Christ has bound together by the bond of charity and love in the time of His precious death,

Nay, also to destroy, profane and pollute what is most sacred therein with a most execrable mind, filthy tongue and detestable touch.

If he gave any hopes of cure in himself or any sign of amendment, he would thereby move all people to regard disposition and to endeavour, by all good means possible, to heal him and to restore him to soundness of mind, so that he might again revoke the heresies he has broached.

Indeed, so far I see in him all the signs that precede death.

I am not moved to think thus because of his disease - however mortal it may be - but rather by his admitting of no medicine, nor any manual operation of the surgeon.

How can he be cured if he will not allow himself to be handled?

In what manner is he to be dealt with, if when you teach him he trifles with you?

If you advise him, he is angry? If you exhort him, he resists? If you would appease him in anything, he is incensed? If you resist him, he is mad?

Otherwise, if he could be cured, what has the pious Vicar of Christ omitted to do, who, in following the example of a good Shepherd, would seek, find, take on his shoulders and bring home this lost sheep to the fold?

But, alas! The greediest wolf of hell has surprised, devoured and swallowed him down into the lowest part of his belly, where he lies half alive and half dead in death.

And, while the pious Pastor calls Luther and bewails the loss of this sheep, Luther belches out of the filthy mouth of the hellish wolf these foul invectives, which the ears of the whole flock do detest, disdain and abhor.

First of all, being unprovoked in any manner, he proposed some articles on Indulgences in which, under pretence of godliness, he most impiously defamed the Pope.

Afterwards, so that he might cast the greater aspersion on the Pope, he conveys them to Rome under the pretence of honour and duty, as if submitting himself to the Pope's Judgment.

Luther enlarged his articles with declarations, much worse than the articles themselves.

Thus, it would appear to everyone that the Pope would not be counselled by a good and pious man, but rather derided by a knavish *little brother*; as if the Pope were so stupid as to hold such an insolence for an honour, as the like of it had never been heard before.

If the Pope deserved no ill, why has this degenerate son cast a false and undeserving scandal on his father?

If anything had been done in Rome which needed reforming, and if Luther had been an honest man and a zealous Christian - as he wishes to be accounted - he would not have preferred his own private glory before the public good of all others.

He would not have desired to have the credit of a scorner among the wicked, laughing at the nakedness of his sleeping father, (Gen 9:22 & ff) uncovering it and pointing at it with his finger.

On the contrary, he would have covered it and advised him more privately with personal letters, following the example of the Apostle who commands us not to deride or reproach our superiors, but to seek them (1 Tim 5:1).

If Luther had done this, I do not doubt that the holy Pope - so well-known for his great benignity to all men - being awakened, would have blessed his Son Japheth, rendered him thanks for his piety and not cursed him in his anger.

When Luther mocked him, the Pope refrained from cursing him.

Rather, like most honourable men, in whose presence Luther was not worthy to appear – the Pope, pitying the miserable, tenderly dealt with him as toward a son instead of a scoffer, so that Luther might desist from his iniquity.

He was so far from obeying the Pope's pious and wholesome counsel that he not only derided the legate - who was so careful for Luther's salvation - but also immediately published another book in which he endeavoured to overthrow the Pope's power.

Thereafter, he was summoned to Rome that he might either render reasons of his writings or recant what he had inconsiderately written.

For his safe passage, every security imaginable was offered to him that he should not undergo the punishment which he deserved, along with sufficient expenses offered him for his journey.

Yet, for all this, this silly *brother*, to show his great modesty and obedience to the Pope, refused to go unless equipped like a king and guarded by a warlike army.

This wary man made his appeal to a general Council - yet not just to any Council, but to one as should next meet in the Holy Ghost.

Thus, in whatsoever Council he might be condemned, he could deny the Holy Ghost to be present in it.

This *holy and spiritual man* denies the Holy Ghost to be anywhere except in his own bosom.

Therefore, after having advised Luther many times to repent from his wickedness, the most conscientious Shepherd has at length been forced to cast out from the fold that sheep infected with an incurable disease - lest the sound sheep be corrupted by contact.

Like David, he deplores the death of his son Absalom, whose life he is unable to save while he sees him hanging from a tree by his beautiful hair, of which he had grown stupidly proud (2 Kgs 18:9).

Thus Luther, realising himself to be cast out from the society of the faithful, began to do what the lamented wicked ones do, viz., when they have fallen into contempt, they contemn (Prov. 18:3).

He has not uttered a groan, nor bewailed his case in which, exalted like Lucifer, he has fallen like lightning (Lk 10:18) and wrought damage.

Having imitated the despair of the devil – being himself a devil too, that is, having become a calumniator - he has begun to rush into blasphemies and calumnies against the Pope.

Like the old serpent (Gen 3), in his jealousy of others who are faithful, Luther has set up nets of infidelity so that he might lure them to taste of the forbidden tree of harmful knowledge and be driven out of the paradise of the Church - from whence he had fallen - into an earth bringing forth thorns and briars.

I indeed abhor this man's great madness and most lamentable state and I wish that even now - God inspiring him by grace - he may at length come to his senses, be converted and live.

I do not wish his conversion as much for his own sake – as much as I wish all to be saved, if possible – as for the grace that, like the prodigal son (Lk 15) in returning and confessing his error to so benign a Father, he may recall anyone whom he has led into error.

However, if he has sunken so deep in the mire that now the sink of impiety and despair shuts its mouth upon him (Ps 68), let him bleat, blaspheme, calumniate and act as a madman, so that *'he that is filthy, let him be filthy still'* (Apoc. 22).

I beseech and entreat all other Christians, by the Heart of Christ, Whose Faith we profess, to turn their ears away from those impious words and not foster schisms and discords, especially at this time when it behoves Christians most particularly to be united against the enemies of Christ.

Do not listen to the insults and detractions against the Vicar of Christ which the fury of the little monk spews up against the Pope; nor contaminate breasts sacred to Christ with impious heresies.

If one sows these he has no charity, swells with vain glory, loses his reason, and burns with envy.

Finally, just as Christians stand together against any infidel anywhere, they should stand together with the same feelings against this one little monk, weak in strength, but in temper more harmful than all infidels anywhere.

The End

Credo in Unam, Sanctam, Catholicam et Apostolicam Ecclesiam

(Creed of Nicea, 325 AD)

1. **Christ established here on earth only one Church** and instituted it as a visible and spiritual community. From its beginning and throughout the centuries has always existed and will always exist, and in which alone are found all the elements that Christ himself instituted. This one Church of Christ, which we confess in the Creed as one, holy, catholic and apostolic [is] constituted and organized in this world as a society, subsists in the Catholic Church, governed by the successor of Peter and the Bishops in communion with him.
2. 'Subsistence' means this perduring, historical continuity and the permanence of **all the elements instituted by Christ in the Catholic Church**, in which the Church of Christ is concretely found on this earth.
3. The word "subsists" **can only be attributed to the Catholic Church alone** precisely because it refers to the mark of unity that we profess in the symbols of the faith ; and this "one" Church subsists in the Catholic Church.
4. The oriental Churches separated from full communion with the Catholic Church, **although separated, have true sacraments and above all – because of the apostolic succession** – the priesthood and the Eucharist.
5. However, since communion with the Catholic Church, the visible head of which is the Bishop of Rome and the Successor of Peter, is not some external complement to a particular Church but rather one of its internal constitutive principles, **these venerable Christian communities lack something in their condition as particular churches**.
6. According to Catholic doctrine, **the Christian Communities born out of the Reformation of the sixteenth century do not enjoy Apostolic Succession** in the sacrament of Orders, and are, therefore, deprived of a constitutive element of the Church.
7. These ecclesial Communities which, specifically because of the absence of the sacramental priesthood, **have not preserved the genuine and integral substance of the Eucharistic Mystery** cannot, according to Catholic doctrine, be called "Churches" in the proper sense.

Excerpts from the Document by the Vatican Congregation for the Doctrine of the Faith published on 29 June 2007, the Solemnity of the Holy Apostles Peter and Paul. The Supreme Pontiff Benedict XVI, at the Audience granted to William Cardinal Levada, Prefect of the Congregation for the Doctrine of the Faith, ratified and confirmed these teachings, adopted in the Plenary Session of the Congregation, and ordered their publication. See full text in the Vatican website: www.Vatican.va

TO OUR FELLOW CATHOLICS

GENERALLY, HENRY VIII is remembered, especially among us Catholics, as the *roué*, the adulterer, the *divorcé*, the wife-killer, the iconoclast, the persecutor of those who remained faithful to Rome, the confiscator of Church property, and with it all, and because of it all, he became a schismatic, the head of a schism, dragging his subjects away from Catholic unity, and making them acknowledge him not only their earthly king, but their spiritual head as well.

And yet it is also true that at least once he had been the *beau-ideal* Henry: in body, tall, straight, broad-shouldered, a master of every gentlemanly accomplishment; in mind naturally clever, an accomplished linguist, musically talented, a learned theologian, and, above all, a faithful son of the Church.

As such he wrote his famous book, *"Assertio septem sacramentorum adversus Martinum Lutherum"* ("Defence of the Seven Sacraments Against Martin Luther").

Lawfully married to Catherine of Aragon, he dallied with the courtesan, Anne Boleyn. Supported by Thomas Cranmer, a follower of Luther, who had been appointed Archbishop of Canterbury, Henry determined to marry Anne at all costs.

Threatened by Pope Clement VII with excommunication, Henry avenged himself by seceding from Rome, and having himself made the head of the Church in England.

However, it is also true that, although he persecuted the Catholics and confiscated their churches and monasteries, Henry insisted on retaining the chief truths of Catholic belief and practice with the exception of dependence on the Holy See, despite Cranmer's efforts to have him embrace Protestantism openly.

Protestantism, however, spread rapidly throughout England in the six years of the reign of Edward VI. Elizabeth I, daughter of Anne Boleyn, rekindled her father's persecution of Catholics. She adopted thirty-nine of Cranmer's forty-two articles, and made the Church a puppet of royalty. She may truthfully be called the real founder of the Anglican Church.

Thus, to this day, the coronation oath includes the affirmation to *"maintain in the United Kingdom the Protestant Reformed Religion established by law."*

What a great moment in History it would be, if, or hopefully *when*, four and a half centuries after *the Island of the Saints* severed ties with the Sacraments that its Royal *Defender of the Faith* affirmed in so stern a manner, sons and daughters of England were to reaffirm them, and bring *Our Lady's Dowry* back home to Rome.

England would enter History as the usher of authentic Christian unity in Europe, en route to that revitalisation of Christendom to resist the inroads of the enemies of the Cross of Christ.

THE ROOT OF THE CRISIS: THE REVOLUTION

When 'Defence of the Seven Sacraments' was published for the first time, Europe in general was undergoing a gradual but dreadful crisis of Faith and Morals. The Church Herself was not free from it. Corruption and laxity were widespread, even in Rome itself.

Today, when the book is being published for the first time in the new millennium, the crisis afflicting the Church and the remnants of Christendom is immensely worse.

To better understand the nature of the present-day process of de-Christianisation, a brief overview of History is necessary.

In the days of Luther and Henry VIII, Christians in Europe were being fragmented into different religious denominations. The unity of the Christian Faith was broken.

Today the whole Western world is being literally de-Christianised - Christian values have been extirpated from it. Agnosticism, secular humanism and relativism reign supreme and have created a cultural and religious void of apocalyptic magnitude. Not surprisingly, non-Christian religions and cultures, especially Islam, fill up the void left by the widespread apostasy.

As early as 1956 Msgr. Angelo Dell'Acqua, substitute for the Vatican Secretary of State, stated that *"Because of the religious agnosticism of the states,"* there has been *"a decline or almost loss of the sense of the Church in modern society."*

The words of Pius XII about a subtle and mysterious 'enemy' of the Church can fittingly be applied to this process:

"It is to be found everywhere and among everyone; it can be both violent and astute. In these last centuries, it has attempted to disintegrate the intellectual, moral, and social unity in the mysterious organism of Christ. It has sought nature without grace, reason without faith, freedom without authority, and, at times, authority without freedom. It is an "enemy" that has become more and more apparent with an absence of

scruples that still surprises: Christ yes; the Church no! Afterwards: God yes; Christ no! Finally the impious shout: God is dead and, even, God never existed! And behold now the attempt to build the structure of the world on foundations which we do not hesitate to indicate as the main causes of the threat that hangs over humanity: economy without God, law without God, politics without God."[110]

This terrible enemy has a name: It is called the *Revolution*.

As Professor Plínio Corrêa de Oliveira expounds in his masterpiece, *'Revolution and Counter-Revolution'*, since the fourteenth century, a gradual transformation of mentality began to take place in Christian Europe.

The profound cause of that transformation of mentality was an explosion of pride and sensuality that has inspired, not one system, but, rather, a whole chain of ideological systems.

Their wide acceptance gave rise to the three great revolutions in the history of the West: Protestantism, the French Revolution, and Communism.

Pride leads to hatred of all superiority and, thus, to the affirmation that inequality is an evil in itself at all levels, principally at the metaphysical and religious ones. This is the egalitarian aspect of the Revolution.

Sensuality, *per se*, tends to sweep aside all barriers. It does not accept restraints and leads to revolt against all authority and law, divine or human, ecclesiastical or civil. This is the liberal aspect of the Revolution.

In the course of the fifteenth century, it became ever more apparent. The thirst for earthly pleasures became a burning desire. Amusements became more and more frequent and sumptuous, increasingly engrossing men. In dress, manners, language, literature, and art, the growing yearning for a life filled with delights of fancy and the senses produced progressive manifestations of sensuality and sluggishness.

Little by little, the seriousness and austerity of former times lost their value. The whole trend was toward gaiety, affability, and festiveness. Hearts began to shy away from the love of sacrifice, from true devotion to the Cross, and from the aspiration to sanctity and eternal life.

---

[110] Pius XII, allocution to the Union of Men of the Italian Catholic Action on October 12 1952, *Discorsi e radiomessagi di Sua Santita Pio XII*, Tipografia Poliglotta Vaticana, 1953), vo. 14, p. 359.

Chivalry, formerly one of the highest expressions of Christian austerity, became amorous and sentimental. The literature of love invaded all countries. Excesses of luxury and the consequent eagerness for gain spread throughout all social classes.

Penetrating intellectual circles, this moral climate produced clear manifestations of pride, such as a taste for ostentatious and vain disputes, for inconsistent tricks of argument, and for fatuous exhibitions of learning.

It praised old philosophical tendencies over which Scholasticism had triumphed. As the former zeal for the integrity of the Faith waned, these tendencies reappeared in new guises.

The absolutism of legists, who adorned themselves with a conceited knowledge of Roman Law, was favourably received by ambitious princes. And, all the while, in great and small alike, there was a fading of the will of yore to keep the royal power within its proper bounds as in the days of Saint Louis of France and Saint Ferdinand of Castile.

This new state of soul contained a powerful although more or less unacknowledged desire for an order of things fundamentally different from that which had reached its heights in the twelfth and thirteenth centuries.

An exaggerated and often delirious admiration for antiquity served as a means for the expression of this desire. In order to avoid direct confrontations with the old medieval tradition, humanism and the Renaissance frequently sought to relegate the Church, the supernatural, and the moral values of religion to a secondary plane.

At the same time, the human type inspired by the pagan moralists was introduced by these movements as an ideal in Europe. This human type and the culture and civilisation consistent with it were truly the precursors of the greedy, sensual, secularist, and pragmatic man of our days and of the materialistic culture and civilization into which we are sinking deeper and deeper.

Efforts to effect a Christian Renaissance did not manage to crush in the germinal stage the factors that led to the gradual triumph of neo-paganism.

In some parts of Europe, this neo-paganism developed without leading to formal apostasy. It found significant resistance. Even when it became established within souls, it did not dare ask them formally to break with the Faith - at least in the beginning.

However, in other countries, it openly attacked the Church.

Pride begot the spirit of doubt, individual examination and naturalistic interpretation of Scripture. It produced insurrection against ecclesiastical authority, expressed in all sects by the denial of the monarchical character of the Universal Church, that is to say, by a revolt against the Papacy.

Some of the more radical sects also denied what could be called the higher aristocracy of the Church, namely, the bishops, her princes. Others even denied the hierarchical character of the priesthood itself by reducing it to a mere delegation of the people, lauded as the only true holder of priestly power.

On the moral field, the triumph of sensuality was affirmed by the suppression of ecclesiastical celibacy and by the introduction of divorce.

Protestantism was a first Revolution. It implanted, in varying degrees, the spirit of doubt, religious liberalism, and ecclesiastical egalitarianism in the different sects it produced.

The French Revolution came next. It was the triumph of egalitarianism in two fields: the religious field in the form of atheism, speciously labelled as secularism; and the political field through the false maxim that all inequality is an injustice, all authority a danger, and freedom the supreme good.

Communism was the transposition of these maxims to the socioeconomic field.

Thus, in every Western nation, this same de-Christianisation process exerts its undefined but overwhelming sway, producing symptoms of tragic magnitude.

Western Christendom constituted a single whole that transcended the several Christian countries without absorbing them. A crisis occurred within this living unity.

Consequently, Christendom, as a family of officially Catholic states, has long ceased to exist. The Western and Christian peoples are mere remnants of it. And now they are all agonizing under the action of this same de-Christianising process.

Indeed, the order of things that was destroyed was medieval Christendom.

Now, medieval Christendom was not just any order, or merely one of many possible orders. It was the realization, in the circumstances inherent to the times and places, of the only authentic order among men, namely, Christian Civilisation.

In his encyclical *Immortale Dei*, Leo XIII described medieval Christendom in these terms:

'There was a time when the philosophy of the Gospel governed the states. In that epoch, the influence of Christian wisdom and its divine virtue permeated the laws, institutions, and customs of the peoples, all categories and all relations of civil society.

'Then the religion instituted by Jesus Christ, solidly established in the degree of dignity due to it, flourished everywhere thanks to the favour of princes and the legitimate protection of magistrates.

'Then the Priesthood and the Empire were united in a happy concord and by the friendly interchange of good offices. So organised, civil society gave fruits superior to all expectations, whose memory subsists and will subsist, registered as it is in innumerable documents that no artifice of the adversaries can destroy or obscure.' [111]

There can be no Christian order without the knowledge and observance of the Law of God. Civilization and culture par excellence are only possible within the fold of the Holy Church. Indeed, as Saint Pius X stated, civilisation...

"Is all the more true, all the more lasting, all the more fecund in precious fruits, the more purely Christian it is; it is all the more decadent, to the great misfortune of society, the further it withdraws from the Christian ideal. Thus, by the intrinsic nature of things, the Church becomes also in fact the guardian and protector of Christian Civilization." [112]

---

[111] Leo XII, encyclical *Immortale Dei*, November 1, 1885, Bonne Presse, Paris, vol. 2, p. 39.

[112] St Pius X, Encyclical *Il fermo proposito*, June 11, 1905, Bonne Presse, Paris, vol. 2, p. 92.

A Catholic Book

It is from this overall perspective that our fellow-Catholics are invited to study and promote this short treatise on the Sacraments, authored by a Catholic King, Henry VIII; acclaimed by a Pope, Leo X; and assisted by a Saint and Martyr, Sir Thomas More.

It is to be hoped that his forceful argumentation will elicit in as many Catholics as possible a *Great Return* to the knowledge and zeal for the purity of the Catholic Faith, Morals and authentic Sacramental life. Such a return is a condition *sine qua non* for the re-Christianisation of Europe and the Western world in general.

However, it is to be feared that no authentic renewal of the Christian Faith and Culture will ever take place as long as all baptised Christians remain disunited.

Pope John Paul II wrote a famous encyclical to encourage unity of Christians – *Ut unum sint*, i.e. that they may be one. In publishing Henry VIII's book we add a small but important qualification: *Ut unum in veritate sint* – that they may be one *in the Truth*.

The Crisis in the Church

The sad reality is that the Catholic Church Herself needs renewal in our times, and urgently so, weakened as She has been by the dreadful crisis that has plagued Her in the aftermath of the Vatican II Council.

It would suffice to read the *Ratzinger Report*, by His Eminence Joseph Cardinal Ratzinger, now our Supreme Pontiff Benedict XVI, to understand the crisis of the Faith that afflicts a large number of bishops, priests and laity in the Church in our times.

Sadly, but truly, it must be acknowledged that the process of de-Christianisation which plagues all Christian countries has even penetrated the sanctuary of the Church. Pope Paul VI called it the *'Smoke of Satan'*.

Again, Professor Plínio Corrêa de Oliveira described the Crisis in *'Revolution and Counter-Revolution'* by quoting the most unsuspected sources.

With an unbelievable momentum, this smoke has spread itself within the Church, similar to the terrible force of poisonous gases in expansion. To the scandal of uncountable souls, the Mystical Body of Christ entered a sinister process of self-destruction, as it were.

Paul VI, in an allocution to the students of the Pontifical Lombard Seminary on December 7, 1968, affirmed:

"The Church finds herself in an hour of disquiet, of self-criticism, one might even say of self-destruction. It is like an acute and complex interior upheaval, which no one expected after the Council. One thought of a blossoming, a serene expansion of the mature concepts of the Council. ... The Church is also being wounded by those who are part of her." [113]

`Later on, in the allocution *Resistite fortes in fide*, June 29, 1972, with greater precision, he explained the calamities in the post-Conciliar phase of the Church. We quote the *Poliglotta Vaticana:*

"Referring to the situation of the Church today, the Holy Father affirmed that he had the feeling that The smoke of Satan has entered into the temple of God through some crack.'

"There is doubt, uncertainty, complexity, restlessness, dissatisfaction, confrontation. People no longer trust the Church; they trust the first secular profane prophet who speaks to us through some newspaper or social movement, running after him and asking him if he has the formula of true life.

"We do not realise that we are already owners and masters of it. Doubt has entered our consciences through windows that ought to be open to the light.... This state of uncertainty also reigns in the Church.

"It was thought that after the Council the history of the Church would enter a sunny day. It entered instead a cloudy, stormy, dark, skeptical, and uncertain day. We preach ecumenism and yet we ourselves are further and further apart. We seek to dig abysses instead of filling them.

---

[113] *Insegnamenti di Paolo VI*, vol. 10, pp. 707-709.

"How did this happen? The Pope confided one of his opinions: An adverse power has intervened. His name is the devil, the mysterious being to which Saint Peter also alludes in his Epistle."

Pope John Paul II also painted a rather sombre picture of the Church's situation:

"One must be realistic and acknowledge with a deep and pained sentiment that a great party of today's Christians feel lost, confused, perplexed, and even disillusioned: ideas contradicting the revealed and unchanging Truth have been spread far and wide; outright heresies in the dogmatic and moral fields have been disseminated, creating doubt, confusion, and rebellion; even the liturgy has been altered.
"Immersed in intellectual and moral "relativism" and therefore in permissiveness, Christians are tempted by atheism, agnosticism, a vaguely moralistic illuminism, a sociological Christianity, without defined dogmas and without objective morality." [114]

Similarly, Joseph Cardinal Ratzinger, the then Prefect of the Congregation for the Doctrine for the Faith, stated:

"Results since the Council seem to be in cruel contrast to the expectations of all, beginning with those of John XXIII and Paul VI. The Popes and the Council Fathers were expecting a new Catholic unity, and instead one has encountered a dissension that - to use the words of Paul VI - seems to have gone from self-criticism to self-destruction. A new enthusiasm was expected, but too often there has been boredom and discouragement instead. A new leap forward was expected, but instead we find ourselves facing a process of progressive decadence.... It must be clearly stated that a real reform of the Church presupposes an unequivocal turning away from the erroneous paths that led to indisputably negative consequences." [115]

---

[114] Allocution to the religious and priests participating in the First Italian National Congress on Missions to the People for the 80s, February 6, 1981, *L'Osservatore Romano*, February 7, 1981.

[115] From Vittorio Messori, Vittorio Messori a colloquio con il cardinale Joseph Ratzinger- *Rapporto sulla fede*, Milan: Edizioni Paoline, 1985, pp. 27-28.

'It is painful to say this. But, in this sense, the evidence singles out the Second Vatican Council as one of the greatest calamities, if not the greatest, in the history of the Church. From the Council on, the *'smoke of Satan'* penetrated the Church in unbelievable proportions. And this smoke is spreading day by day, with the terrible force of gases in expansion. To the scandal of uncountable souls, the Mystical Body of Christ entered a sinister process of self-destruction, as it were.' (*Revolution and Counter-Revolution*, part III, Chapter 2).

TRUE AND FALSE ECUMENISM

Perhaps one of the greatest enemies of the Faith today, and which prevents the authentic renewal of the Church and reunion of all Christians in the Truth, is a certain false ecumenism, soaked with irenic relativism, which, forcing itself in a truly dictatorial manner, aims to gather together all faiths into one single people, instead of all peoples into one single Faith.

The Catholic Catechism is clear in regards the mission of the Church:

"*Christ sent his Apostles so that repentance and forgiveness of sins should be preached in his name to all nations. 'Go therefore and* **make disciples of all nations**, *baptising them in the name of the Father and of the Son and of the Holy Spirit.' The mission to baptise, and so the sacramental mission, is implied in the mission to evangelise, because the sacrament is prepared for by the word of God and by the faith which is assent to this word.*" (CCC 1122)

The commandment of the Son of God to His Apostles is to *make disciples of all nations*, to teach them to observe all things whatsoever He had commanded them.

He commanded them to *evangelise* the peoples of the world – not to *'ecumenise'* with their religions without intending to bring about conversion. That would make His commandment totally void.

To convert them to Him in *His terms*, not to accept their sincerity as sufficient proof of truth or legitimacy.

Such false ecumenism has no foundation whatsoever in either Sacred Scripture or the Apostolic Tradition. It is one of those man-made, counterfeit *'traditions'*, which Our Lord rebuked so sternly in the

Gospels, when He said, *"You make void the commandment of God, that you may keep your own tradition."* (Mk 7:9)

Again, the Catholic Catechism teaches:

*"The Church's faith precedes the faith of **the believer who is invited to adhere to it**. When the Church celebrates the sacraments, she confesses **the faith received from the Apostles** - whence the ancient saying: lex orandi, lex credendi - the law of prayer is the law of faith: the Church believes as she prays. Liturgy is a constitutive element of the holy and living Tradition".* (CCC 1124)

Our Divine Saviour wanted His Church to be a preaching, expanding, missionary Church, presenting the objective truth with both charity and fearlessness; not a dialoguing, shrinking, maintenance Church, presenting views and opinions for discussion.

Such would be a mere exercise in relativism, which is abhorrent to the Mind of Christ.

Doctrinal relativism is certainly one of the main – if not the main – enemy of salvation in our times, both as Christian nations and individuals.

At the homily of the Conclave that elected him Pope, Cardinal Ratzinger outlined the problem and proposed the solution when he said that *the dictatorship of relativism* is confronting the world.

This dictatorship does not recognise anything as absolute and leaves the ultimate measure only the measure of each one and his desires. This relativism is seen as the only behaviour abreast of our times. Christians, however, have another measure, which is the son of God true Man.

He emphasised that mature faith does not follow fashion and the latest novelty, but is profoundly rooted in friendship with Christ. Catholics cannot remain immature in the faith, in a state of inferiority, as they run the risk of being tossed about and carried here and there by any doctrinal wind. ... A clear faith, according to the creed of the Church, is needed.

His predecessor John Paul II certainly outlined the Mind of the Son of God True Man and the desired maturity in the Faith when he addressed the Spanish youth in 1981:

"Learn to think, speak and act in accordance with the evangelical simplicity and clarity: yes, yes; no, no'. Learn to call black, black; and white, white. Learn to call good, good; and evil, evil. To call sin, sin, and not to call it 'progress', or 'liberation', even if fashion and propaganda are opposed to this teaching".

The final goal of true ecumenism is to gather the whole world under *'One Lord, one Faith, one Baptism'* (Eph. 4:5) in the one *'Church of Christ, the Pillar and mainstay of the Truth'* (1 Tim 3:15).

Let us dialogue and discuss issues, yes, by all means – but if the final goal is missed, if we make compromise in the truths of the Faith, everything will have been in vain.

As Pope John Paul II taught, *"In matters of faith, compromise is in contradiction with God who is Truth"* (*Ut Unum Sint*).

Perhaps the Pontiff was echoing Blessed Pius IX, the last Pope-King who was beatified by the same John Paul II and whose sacred relics today repose in St Peter's Basilica awaiting the great Day of the Resurrection. He prophetically pointed out that...

'Though the children of this world may be wiser than the children of light, their snares and their violence would undoubtedly have less success if a great number of those who call themselves Catholics did not extend a friendly hand to them.

'Yes, unfortunately, there are those who seem to want to walk in agreement with our enemies and try to build an alliance between light and darkness, an accord between justice and iniquity, by means of those so-called liberal Catholic doctrines, which, based on the most pernicious principles, adulate the civil power when it invades things spiritual and urge souls to respect or at least tolerate the most iniquitous laws, as if it had not been written absolutely that no one can serve two masters.

'They are certainly much more dangerous and more baneful than our declared enemies, not only because they second their efforts, perhaps without realising it, but also because, by maintaining themselves at the very edge of condemned opinions, they take on an appearance of integrity and irreprehensible doctrine, beguiling the imprudent friends of conciliations and deceiving honest persons, who would revolt against a declared error. 'In this way, they divide the minds, rend the unity, and weaken the forces that should be assembled against the enemy." [116]

---

[116] Pius IX, letter to the president and members of the Saint Ambrose Circle of Milan, March 6, 1873, in *I Papi e La Gioventù*, Rome, Editrice A.V.E., 1944), p. 36)

The publication of *'Defence of the Seven Sacraments'* is an unpretentious contribution to help reduce the present-day *immaturity in the Faith* among Catholics, and do away with the *state of inferiority* that plagues so many in the quagmire of today's false ecumenism.

Henry VIII aimed to bring about unity among Christians: not just any unity, but *a clear Unity in the Truth*, to which he called all Christians of his time to stand up and be counted for the Faith of the Apostles and the Sacraments of the Church of Jesus Christ.

"Truth enlightens man's intelligence and shapes his freedom, leading him to know and love the Lord" (John Paul II, *Veritatis Splendor*).

The publication of 'Defence *of the Seven Sacraments'* is also aimed to encourage faithful Catholics of every walk of life to heed the call of John Paul II to help *'re-evangelise the baptised'*.

May the attentive study of Henry VIII's masterpiece be a great incentive to faithful Catholics the world over to promote the Apostolic teaching on the ordinary means of receiving divine grace, so that, strengthened by them, we may proclaim the truths of the Gospel of Jesus Christ and authentic Christian unity in the Church founded by Him – en route to our heavenly Fatherland.

Ut unum sint - ut unum in veritate sint.

To Our Separated Brethren in Baptism

OUR SEPARATED BRETHREN belonging to the Anglican, Baptist, Congregational, Episcopalian, Lutheran, Presbyterian, Methodist and all other Protestant denominations that have emerged from or after Martin Luther's Revolution are cordially invited to attentively read 'Defence of the Seven Sacraments' by King Henry VIII.

In his unique work, Henry argues from the standpoints of Sacred Scripture, the writings of the early Fathers of the Church, the Faith of the Universal Church, the consent of so many ages and peoples as well as commonsense itself.

His language is imbued with theological thinking, as one would naturally expect in a work of such nature. And yet it is simple and straightforward, coming from a heart zealous for the integrity of the Truth. His command of Sacred Scripture, both the Old and the New Testaments, is second to none.

His knowledge of the early Fathers' writings is remarkably vast and shows, without a shadow of a doubt, the authentic beliefs of the early Christians regarding the seven Sacraments.

Occasionally, Henry's characteristic zeal to defend the Faith encumbered the clarity of the nuances he wished to convey.

Also, at times, his terminology may appear somewhat too aggressive, scornful, and perhaps even abusive, towards Luther; or one might accuse

Henry of addressing Luther in the same insulting, offensive language Luther used against the Church of Rome.

In any event, we trust Henry's passionate zeal will be forgiven by men of good will, if one considers how horrifying it was for him to witness the marvellous unity of the Church of Jesus Christ and Christendom being torn apart by doctrinal and moral dissent in his own lifetime.

* * *

Albeit in different ways, the truth is that in these distressing days in which we live, marked by unbridled violence, unrest, anguish and hopelessness for so many, Europe and the whole Western world are suffering from the alarming process of de-Christianisation we are very much familiar with.

Secular humanism, materialism and hedonism – among other factors – have brought about the extirpation of Christian values from every other sphere of human endeavour.

As Pope Pius XII accurately observed, this process of de-Christianisation *'is an 'enemy' that has become more and more apparent with an absence of scruples that still surprises: Christ yes; the Church no! Afterwards: God yes; Christ no! Finally the impious shout: God is dead and, even, God never existed! And behold now the attempt to build the structure of the world on foundations which we do not hesitate to indicate as the main causes of the threat that hangs over humanity: economy without God, law without God, politics without God.'* [117]

As a direct consequence of this process, the West - particularly Europe - is gradually being emptied of Christian peoples and values.

The result is there for all to see: peoples without Christian Baptism and with strong proselytising zeal gradually fill up the populational, cultural and religious vacuum.

Lured by the mirage of economic growth and prosperity, the one time cradle of Christian Civilisation is sliding towards a dangerous quagmire of humanistic apathy, punctuated by growing fires of Islamic fervour.

It can be said without fear of contradiction that the Episcopal ordination of women and of practicing homosexuals has not helped the

---

[117] Pius XII, allocution to the Union of Men of the Italian Catholic Action on October 12 1952, *Discorsi e radiomessagi di Sua Santita Pio XII* (Vatican: Tipografia Poliglotta Vaticana, 1953), vo. 14, p. 359.

proclamation of the authentic Gospel of Jesus Christ. The ensuing divisions among Protestant denominations on these issues leave no room for doubt that such course of action will have catastrophic results.

A genuine unity of Christians is undoubtedly called for, as a matter of consequence and survival, so that the Religion of Jesus Christ may advance and flourish in a visible and dynamic manner, for the glory of God, salvation of souls and greater good of all mankind.

REBUILDING THE CITY TOGETHER

We do not think even for a moment that the return of our separated brethren to full communion with the Apostolic See of Rome could be likened to the parable of the prodigal son. A major difference exists.

The prodigal son, after a life of sin away from his paternal home, returned to a house ready to receive him back with great jubilation in the Lord. At home he found order, peace, abundance and happiness.

Such is arguably not the case with the Catholic Church today. From the words of Paul VI, John Paul II and Cardinal Ratzinger cited in the previous chapter in this study *('To our fellow-Catholics')*, the return of our separated brethren from all Protestant denominations - especially the Church of England - might rather be likened in a sense to the return of the Jews from the Babylonian exile: the Jews found their religion in crisis, their Temple emptied of its former glory, the holy city of Jerusalem largely destroyed and inhabited by a mixture of zealous and lukewarm Jews, alongside the irenic Samaritans.

And yet, in spite of what they saw, **they knew they were coming home.**

The returning Jews rebuilt the Temple and the city together with the local Jews who had remained faithful, and refused the Samaritans' involvement.

Making all due allowances for the different situations, one may say that now it may be the time when our returning brethren are called to work together with faithful Catholics to restore the Church of Christ to her original splendour, en route to rebuild Christian Civilisation both in Europe and in all countries formed under the sign of the Cross of Christ.

Like the mustard seed of the parable, it is to be hoped that the publication of the New Millennium edition of the *'Defence of the Seven Sacraments'* may be a meaningful contribution towards such a noble purpose.

History tells us that when men resolve to cooperate with the grace of God, great marvels are worked: the conversion of the Roman Empire; the formation of the Middle Ages; the Reconquest of Spain - starting from Covadonga. These and all the events result from the great resurrections of soul of which people are capable. These resurrections are invincible, because nothing can defeat people who are virtuous and who truly love God.

This will surely happen again, when all those who claim the name Christian will unreservedly profess the fullness of the teachings left to the Apostles by Him who is the Way, the Truth and the Life - Christ our Lord and King - in the unity of the one Church He founded: the One, Holy, Catholic and Apostolic Church, our Mother, Ark of Salvation and Gate of Heaven, *Pillar and Mainstay of the Truth* (1 Tim 3:15)

On the "Dictatorship of Relativism"

Joseph Cardinal Ratzinger

(Excerpts from the Homily at the Mass of the Conclave that elected him Pope)

"We would have to speak of the 'measure of the fullness of Christ,' which we are called to attain to truly be adults in the faith. We should not remain as children in the faith, in the state of minors.

And what does it mean to be children in the faith?

St. Paul answers: It means to be *'tossed to and from and carried about with every wind of doctrine'* (Ephesians 4:14).

A very timely description!

How many winds of doctrine we have known in these last decades, how many ideological currents, how many fashions of thought? The small boat of thought of many Christians has often remained agitated by the waves, tossed from one extreme to the other: from Marxism to liberalism, to libertinism; from collectivism to radical individualism; from atheism to a vague religious mysticism; from agnosticism to syncretism, etc.

Every day new sects are born and we see realised what St. Paul says on the deception of men, on the cunning that tends to lead into error (cf. Ephesians 4:14). To have a clear faith, according to the creed of the Church, is often labelled as fundamentalism.

While relativism, that is, allowing oneself to be carried about with every wind of 'doctrine,' seems to be the only attitude that is fashionable. A dictatorship of relativism is being constituted that recognises nothing as absolute and which only leaves the 'I' and its whims as the ultimate measure.

We have another measure: the Son of God, true man. He is the measure of true humanism. 'Adult' is not a faith that follows the waves in fashion and the latest novelty. Adult and mature is a faith profoundly rooted in friendship with Christ.

This friendship opens us to all that is good and gives us the measure to discern between what is true and what is false, between deceit and truth.

We must mature in this adult faith; we must lead the flock of Christ to this faith. And this faith, the only faith, creates unity and takes place in charity.

St. Paul offers us a beautiful phrase, in opposition to the continual ups and downs of those who are like children tossed by the waves, to bring about truth in charity, as fundamental formula of Christian existence.

Truth and charity coincide in Christ. In the measure that we come close to Christ, also in our life, truth and charity are fused.

Charity without truth would be blind; truth without charity would be like 'a clanging cymbal' (1 Corinthians 13:1).

[In the Gospel] The Lord addresses these wonderful words to us: *'No longer do I call you servants ... but I have called you friends'* (John 15:15). Many times we simply feel like useless servants, and it is true (cf. Luke 17:10).

And, despite this, the Lord calls us *friends*; he makes us his friends; he gives us his friendship. The Lord defines friendship in two ways. There are no secrets between friends: Christ tells us everything he hears from the Father; he gives us his full confidence and, with confidence, also knowledge.

He reveals his face to us, his heart. He shows us his tenderness for us, his passionate love that goes to the folly of the cross.

He gives us his confidence; he gives us the power to speak with his 'I': *'This is my body,'* and *'I absolve you.'* He entrusts his body to us, the

Church. He entrusts his truth to our weak minds, our weak hands, the mystery of God the Father, Son and Holy Spirit; the mystery of the God who *'so loved the world that he gave his only Son'* (John 3:16). He has made us his friends and, we, how do we respond?

The second element with which Jesus defines friendship is the communion of wills. *'Idem velle - idem nolle,'* was also for Romans the definition of friendship. *'You are my friends if you do what I command you'* (John 15:14).

Friendship with Christ coincides with what the third petition of the Our Father expresses: *'Thy will be done, on earth as it is in heaven.'* In the hour of Gethsemane, Jesus transformed our rebellious human will in a will conformed and united with the divine will.

He suffered all the drama of our autonomy and, in carrying our will in God's hands, he gave us true freedom: *'Nevertheless, not as I will, but as you will'* (Matthew 26:39).

In this communion of wills our redemption takes place: to be friends of Jesus, to become friends of God. The more we love Jesus, the more we know him, and the more our genuine freedom grows, as well as the joy of being redeemed.

Thank you, Jesus, for your friendship!

The other element of the Gospel that I would like to mention is Jesus' discourse on bearing fruit:

'I [...] chose you and appointed you to go and bear fruit that will remain' (John 15:16). Here the dynamism of the Christian's existence appears, of the apostle: *'I appointed you to go.'* We must be animated by a 'holy anxiety,' the anxiety of taking the gift of faith, of friendship with Christ, to all. In truth, love, friendship with God, has been given to us so that it will also reach others.

We have received the faith to give it to others; we are priests to serve others. And we must bear fruit that abides. But, what abides? Money does not last. Buildings do not last, or books.

After a certain time, more or less long, all this disappears. The only thing that abides eternally is the human soul - man created by God for eternity.

The fruit that abides, therefore, is the one we have sown in human souls, love, knowledge; the gesture capable of touching the heart; the word that opens the soul to the joy of the Lord.

So, let us go and ask the Lord to help us to bear fruit, a fruit that abides. Only thus is the earth transformed from a vale of tears into a garden of God."

Highlights of Cardinal Ratzinger's teaching:

1. The *dictatorship of relativism* is confronting the world.
2. This dictatorship does not recognise anything as absolute and leaves the ultimate measure only the measure of each one and his desires.
3. This relativism is seen as the only behaviour abreast of our times.
4. Christians, however, have another measure, which is the son of God true Man.
5. Mature faith does not follow fashion and the latest novelty, but is profoundly rooted in friendship with Christ.
6. Catholics cannot remain immature in the faith, in a state of inferiority, as they run the risk of being tossed about and carried here and there by any doctrinal wind.
7. Friendship with Christ coincides with what the third petition of the Our Father expresses: *'Thy will be done, on earth as it is in heaven.'*
8. A clear faith, according to the creed of the Church, is needed.

This clarity of thinking was outlined by His predecessor when he addressed the Spanish youth in 1981.

John Paul II said:

"Learn to think, speak and act in accordance with the evangelical simplicity and clarity: yes, yes; no, no'. Learn to call black, black; and white, white. Learn to call good, good; and evil, evil. To call sin, sin, and not to call it 'progress', or 'liberation', even if fashion and propaganda are opposed to this teaching".

How can one learn to think, speak and act in this way?

In his masterpiece *'Revolution and Counter-Revolution'*, Plínio Corrêa de Oliveira proposes eight ways to revive the notions of good and evil in our days:

1. Avoid all formulations that smack of secular or inter-denominational morality, because secularism and inter-denominationalism logically lead to amorality.

2. Opportunely point out that God has the right to be obeyed and that, therefore, His Commandments are true laws, which we ought to observe in the spirit of obedience and not simply because they please us.

3. Emphasise that the law of God is intrinsically good and in accordance with the order of the universe, in which the perfection of the Creator is mirrored. For this reason, the Law of God should not only be obeyed, but loved; and evil should not only be shunned, but hated.

4. Promote the notions of reward and of chastisement after death.

5. Favour social customs and laws in which uprightness is honoured and wickedness suffers public sanctions.

6. Favour customs and laws meant to prevent proximate occasions of sin and even those conditions that, having the mere appearance of evil, may be harmful to public morality.

7. Insist on the effects of Original Sin in man, his frailty, the fruitfulness of the Redemption by Our Lord Jesus Christ, and the need for grace, prayer, and vigilance in order for man to persevere.

8. Make use of every opportunity to draw attention to the mission of the Church as teacher of virtue, fountain of grace, and the irreconcilable enemy of error and sin.

If both spiritual and temporal leaders were to put these suggestions into practice, one may surely expect great spiritual fruits in individual souls as well as a true *metanoia* in society at large.

Apostolic Letter
Amantissima voluntatis
(To the English people)
Pope Leo XIII
27 April 1895
(Excerpts)

We have greatly desired to give to the illustrious English race a token of Our sincere affection. This wish has been kept alive by the hearty goodwill We have always felt towards your people, whose great deeds in olden times the history of the Church declares.

We were yet more moved by not infrequent conversations with your countrymen, who testified to their anxiety for *peace and eternal salvation through unity of faith.*

God is Our witness how keen is Our wish that some effort of Ours might tend to assist and further the great work of obtaining *the reunion of Christendom.*

We have with full consideration determined to invite *all Englishmen who glory in the Christian name* to lift up their hearts to God with Us, to fix their trust in Him, and to seek from Him the help necessary in such a matter by assiduous diligence in holy prayer.

The love and care of the Roman Pontiffs for England has been traditional from the days of Our holy predecessor Gregory the Great.

The English race was in those days devoted to this *centre of Christian unity* divinely constituted in the Roman Bishops, and that in the course of ages men of all ranks were bound to them by ties of loyalty.

But, in the storms which devastated Catholicity throughout Europe in the sixteenth century, England, too, received a grievous wound; for it was first unhappily wrenched from communication with the Apostolic See, and then was bereft of that holy Faith in which for long centuries it had rejoiced and found liberty.

It was a sad defection; and Our predecessors, while lamenting it in their earnest love, made every prudent effort to put an end to it, and to mitigate the many evils consequent upon it.

No thought is more welcome to Our soul than that *happy unity of Faith and wills* for which our Redeemer and divine Master prayed in that earnest supplication - a unity which, if useful at all times even for temporal interests, both at home and abroad, is shown by *the very divisions and confusions of these days* to be more than ever needful.

We on Our part, urged thereto by the example of Christ and the duty of Our Apostolic Office, have not ceased to pray, and still humbly pray, for *the return of Christian nations now divided from Us to the unity of former days*.

In these days Our thoughts turn with love and hope to the English people, observing as We do the frequent and manifest works of divine grace in their midst; how, to some, it is plain, the confusion of religious dissensions which divide them is a cause of deep concern; how *the number of those religious and discreet men, who sincerely labour much for reunion with the Catholic Church, is increasing*.

May all meet into *the unity of Faith and of the knowledge* of the Son of God careful to keep the unity of the Spirit in the bond of peace, one Body and one Spirit; as you are called in one hope of your calling – *'one Lord, one faith, one baptism'* (Eph. 4: 3-5).

With loving heart, then, We turn to you all in England, to whatever community or institution you may belong, desiring *to recall you to this holy unity*.

We beseech you, as you value your eternal salvation, to offer up humble and continuous prayer to God, our Heavenly Father, the giver of all light, who with gentle power impels us to the good and the right; and without ceasing to implore light to know the truth in all its fullness, and *to embrace the designs of His mercy with single and entire faithfulness*, calling upon the glorious name and merits of Jesus Christ.

The time is not far distant when thirteen centuries will have been completed since the English race welcomed those apostolic men sent from this very city of Rome, and, casting aside the pagan deities, dedicated the first fruits of its faith to Christ our Lord and God.

This encourages Our hope.

It is, indeed, an event worthy to be remembered with public thanksgiving; would that this occasion might bring to all reflecting minds the memory of *the faith then preached to your ancestors*, the same which is now preached – *'Jesus Christ yesterday, today, and the same forever'*, as the Apostle says.

We humbly call on St. Gregory, whom the English have ever rejoiced to greet as the Apostle of their race, on Augustine his disciple and his messenger, and on those other Saints of God, through whose wonderful virtues and no less wonderful deeds England has merited the title of *'Island of the Saints'*; on St. Peter and St. George, those special Patrons, and above all on Mary, the Holy Mother of God, whom Christ Himself from the Cross left to be the Mother of mankind, to whom your kingdom was dedicated by your forefathers under that glorious title 'The Dowry of Mary.'

May the divine prayer of Christ Himself for unity fill up the full measure of Our desires, a prayer which on this day, through the mystery of His most holy Resurrection, We repeat with the utmost confidence:

'Holy Father, keep them in Thy name whom Thou hast given Me: that they may be one as We also are one. . . . Sanctify them in truth. Thy word is truth. . . . And not for them only do I pray, but for them also who through their word shall believe in Me: that all may be one, as Thou, Father, in Me, and I in Thee; that they also may be one in Us. . . . I in them and Thou in Me: that they may be made perfect in one: and the world may know that Thou hast sent Me and hast loved them, as Thou hast also loved Me'.

Finally, We desire all manner of blessings from God for the whole of the British people, and with all Our heart We pray that those who seek *the kingdom of Christ and salvation in the unity of Faith* may enter on the full realization of their desires.

Prayers for England, Mary's Dowry

In fulfilment of a vow made in 1381, King Richard II solemnly renewed the offering of England to Mary as Her dowry.

This was done in Westminster Abbey near the shrine of Saint Edward the Confessor who traditionally first offered England to Mary and in whose reign Our Lady appeared in Walsingham in 1061, England's "little Nazareth".

King Richard declared:

> Dos tua Virgo pia, heac est.
> 'This is Thy Dowry, Holy Virgin.'

To the Blessed Virgin
Prayer for our English Brethren

O Blessed Virgin Mary, Mother of God and our most gentle Queen and Mother, look down in mercy upon England thy Dowry and upon us all who greatly hope and trust in thee.

By thee it was that Jesus our Saviour and our hope was given unto the world; and He has given thee to us that we might hope still more. Plead for us thy children, whom thou didst receive and accept at the foot of the Cross.

O sorrowful Mother! Intercede for our separated brethren, that with us in the one true fold they may be united to the supreme Shepherd, the Vicar of thy Son.

Pray for us all, dear Mother that by faith fruitful in good works we may all deserve to see and praise God, together with thee, in our heavenly home. Amen.

"We grant, that is, to all those who piously recite this prayer, to whatever nation they may belong, an indulgence of three hundred days; moreover, a plenary indulgence once a month on the observance of the usual conditions to those who have recited it daily". Pope Leo XIII.

In Latin

Ad Sanctissima Virginem pro Anglis fratribus precatio

O Beata Virgo Maria, Mater Dei, Regina nostra et Mater dulcissima, benigna oculos tuos converte ad Angliam, quae Dos Tua vocatur, converte ad nos, qui magna in Te fiducia confidimus.

Per Te datus est Christus Salvator mundi, in quo spes nostra consisteret; ab ipso autem Tu data es nobis, per quam spes eadem augeretur.

Eia igitur, ora pro nobis, quos Tibi apud Crucem Domini excepisti filios, o perdolens Mater: intercede pro fratribus dissidentibus, ut nobiscum in unico vero Ovili adiungantur summo Pastori, Vicario in terris Filii Tui.

Pro nobis omnibus deprecare, o Mater piissima, ut per fidem, bonis operibus foecundam, mereamur tecum omnes contemplari Deum in caelesti patria et collaudare per saecula. Amen.

Collects of the Mass of the English Martyrs (Traditional)

O God, Who from the very birth of our English Church didst make us the Dowry of the Blessed Virgin Mary, and the subjects of Peter, the Prince of the Apostles; grant graciously that, staunch in the profession of the Catholic Faith, we may ever both cherish that most Blessed Virgin, and remain in obedience unto Peter. Through Christ Our Lord. Amen.

O God, Who from among the orders of the English people didst raise up Thy Blessed Martyrs the Bishop John, Thomas and their companions to fight manfully for the maintenance of the true Faith and of the primacy of the Holy See; do Thou, through their merits and prayers, grant that, by the profession of that same Faith, we may all become and remain one, in accordance with the prayers of Thy Son. Through Christ Our Lord. Amen.

Walsingham Prayer to Our Lady

(From the Pilgrim Manual of the Anglican Shrine)

O Mary, recall the solemn moment when Jesus, Your divine Son, dying on the Cross, confided us to Your maternal care. You are our Mother, we desire ever to remain Your devout Children. Let us therefore feel the effects of Your powerful intercession with Jesus Christ.
Make Your Name again glorious in this place once renowned throughout our land by Your visits, favours and many miracles.
Pray, O holy Mother of God for the conversion of England, restoration of the sick, consolation of the afflicted, repentance of sinners, peace to the departed.
O Blessed Mary, Mother of God, Our Lady of Walsingham, intercede for us. Amen.

Apostolic Letter Issued Motu Proprio Proclaiming Saint Thomas More Patron of Statesman and Politicians

(excerpts)

POPE JOHN PAUL II
FOR PERPETUAL REMEMBRANCE

The life and martyrdom of Saint Thomas More have been the source of a message which spans the centuries and which speaks to people everywhere of the inalienable dignity of the human conscience.

Thomas More had a remarkable political career in his native land. Born in London in 1478 of a respectable family, as a young boy he was placed in the service of the Archbishop of Canterbury, John Morton, Lord Chancellor of the Realm. He then studied law at Oxford and London, while broadening his interests in the spheres of culture, theology and classical literature.

His sincere religious sentiment led him to pursue virtue through the assiduous practice of asceticism: he cultivated friendly relations with the Observant Franciscans of the Friary at Greenwich, and for a time he lived at the London Charterhouse, these being two of the main centres of religious fervour in the Kingdom.

Throughout his life he was an affectionate and faithful husband and father, deeply involved in his children's religious, moral and intellectual education.

Family life also gave him ample opportunity for prayer in common and *lectio divina*, as well as for happy and wholesome relaxation. Thomas attended daily Mass in the parish church, but the austere penances which he practised were known only to his immediate family.

He was elected to Parliament for the first time in 1504. Henry VIII renewed his mandate in 1510, and even made him the Crown's representative in the capital. This launched him on a prominent career in public administration.

Having been made a member of the King's Council, presiding judge of an important tribunal, deputy treasurer and a knight, in 1523 he became Speaker of the House of Commons.

Highly esteemed by everyone for his unfailing moral integrity, sharpness of mind, his open and humorous character, and his extraordinary learning, in 1529 at a time of political and economic crisis in the country he was appointed by the King to the post of Lord Chancellor. The first layman to occupy this position, Thomas faced an extremely difficult period, as he sought to serve King and country.

In 1532, not wishing to support Henry VIII's intention to take control of the Church in England, he resigned. He withdrew from public life, resigning himself to suffering poverty with his family and being deserted by many people who, in the moment of trial, proved to be false friends.

Given his inflexible firmness in rejecting any compromise with his own conscience, in 1534 the King had him imprisoned in the Tower of London, where he was subjected to various kinds of psychological pressure.

Thomas More did not allow himself to waver, and he refused to take the oath requested of him, since this would have involved accepting a political and ecclesiastical arrangement that prepared the way for uncontrolled despotism.

At his trial, he made an impassioned defence of his own convictions on the indissolubility of marriage, the respect due to the juridical patrimony of Christian civilisation, and the freedom of the Church in her relations with the State. Condemned by the Court, he was beheaded.

Saint Thomas More distinguished himself by his constant fidelity to legitimate authority and institutions precisely in his intention to serve not power but the supreme ideal of justice. His life teaches us that government is above all an exercise of virtue.

Unwavering in this rigorous moral stance, this English statesman placed his own public activity at the service of the person, especially if that person was weak or poor; he dealt with social controversies with a superb sense of fairness; he was vigorously committed to favouring and defending the family; he supported the all-round education of the young. His profound detachment from honours and wealth, his serene and joyful humility, his balanced knowledge of human nature and of the vanity of success, his certainty of judgement rooted in faith: these all gave him that confident inner strength that sustained him in adversity and in the face of death. His sanctity shone forth in his martyrdom, but it had been prepared by an entire life of work devoted to God and neighbour.

This harmony between the natural and the supernatural is perhaps the element which more than any other defines the personality of this great English statesman: he lived his intense public life with a simple humility marked by good humour, even at the moment of his execution.

This was the height to which he was led by his passion for the truth. What enlightened his conscience was the sense that man cannot be sundered from God, nor politics from morality.

The life of Saint Thomas More clearly illustrates a fundamental truth of political ethics.

I am confident therefore that the proclamation of the outstanding figure of Saint Thomas More as Patron of Statesmen and Politicians will redound to the good of society.

Blessed and glorified be Jesus Christ, the Redeemer of man, yesterday, today and for ever.

Given at Saint Peter's, on the thirty-first day of October in the year 2000, the twenty-third of my Pontificate.

Iohannes Paulus PP. II

In Memoriam

King Henry's gallant defence of the true Catholic and Apostolic Faith to refute Luther's doctrines gained him a Papal Title: *Fidei Defensor*, Defender of the Faith.

In the course of History, other kings have received titles from the Vicar of Christ, e.g., the French king was titled *Rex Christianissimus,* the Spanish, *Rex Catholicus*; the Portuguese, *Rex Fidelissiumus*; the Hungarian, *Rex Apostolicus*.

Unfortunately, it is an undeniable historical fact that the English Defender of the Faith did not remain in the Faith of the Church he once defended so valiantly.

That notwithstanding, it could also be said that the Papal title was not altogether wasted in Merry England: If the King renounced the Faith he has intrepidly defended, his no less intrepid Lord Chancellor, Sir Thomas More, the celebrated Bishop of Rochester, John Fisher, and over 50 valorous English Martyrs, honoured the title and paid with their lives for their fidelity to the Apostolic teaching, gaining for themselves the glorious crown of martyrdom.

In many ways, History repeats itself.

In the 20th Century, more Catholics died for the Faith than in all the nineteen previous centuries combined. In the Soviet Union, China, The Middle East, Africa, Asia, nearly everywhere, hundreds of thousands of loyal sons and daughters of the Church imitated the fidelity to Jesus Christ lived by Saints Thomas More and John Fisher. These brave martyrs joined the ranks of the early Christians who died out of love of, and fidelity to, our Divine Redeemer.

Nevertheless, there is also another kind of martyrdom that may be seen at times as more painful to endure than the sudden death for Christ: It is the tireless, lifelong work of a missionary, a confessor, a preacher or a layman whose life is dedicated to serve God Our Lord and His Church.

True Defenders of the Faith, they suffer with the Church, at times alone, often misunderstood, and frequently let down by those who ought to give them support. However, they remain steadfastly faithful to God and themselves, unceasingly striving to promote the Kingdom of Christ and dedicate their entire lives to its triumph.

We have been privileged to know one of such men. With profound respect and veneration we mention his name at the close of this study:

Plínio Corrêa de Oliveira

A fervent devotee of the Blessed Virgin Mary, ardent adorer of the Blessed Sacrament and unquestionably faithful to the See of Peter, from his youth on he dedicated his life to the propagation of the Faith and Social Teaching of the Catholic Church, the defence of her unsullied orthodoxy, the combat against her enemies, both within and without.

As a faithful disciple of Our Lord and Saviour Jesus Christ, Plínio Correa de Oliveira had this in common with Sir Thomas More: both were great Catholic intellectuals and writers. They were pious men, but above all laymen who indefatigably worked to encourage everyone to follow the

Divine Master's footsteps in the Church He founded, not fearing to displease those who opposed the supreme rule of the Magisterium.

Accordingly, like Sir Thomas, Plínio Correa de Oliveira was at different times admired, applauded, opposed, calumniated, and betrayed.

His intellectual life has been portrayed in a best-seller, The *'Crusader of the 20th Century'*, authored by the renowned Italian University Professor Roberto de Mattei and published in Rome in 1995. [118]

Plínio Correa de Oliveira wrote several books to defend the Catholic Church. His first work, *'In Defence of Catholic Action'*, written in 1943, was highly praised by the Vatican Substitute Secretary of State, Archbishop Giovanni Montini, on behalf of Pope Pius XII. Cardinal Montini was subsequently elected to the Papal throne as Paul VI.

His great masterpiece, *'Revolution and Counter-Revolution,'* written in 1959, received the praise of Cardinals, Archbishops, Bishops, intellectuals and nobles in various countries.

Perhaps the most outstanding word of praise came from the great Fr. Anastasio Gutierrez, C.M.F., Doctor in Canon Law at the Lateran University, member of the Pontifical Council for the interpretation of Legislative Texts and the great advisor of pope John Paul II on Canon Law, who wrote: *"Revolution and Counter-Revolution is a magisterial book ... a prophetic work in the best sense of the word, whose contents ought to be taught at the superior learning centres in the Church. ... An authentic product of the Sapientia Christiana"*.

Another work, titled *'The Church and the Communist State: The Impossible Coexistence'*, published in 1963, was acclaimed as *'A most faithful echo of the documents of the Supreme Magisterium of the Church'* by Cardinals Pizzardo and Staffa, respectively Prefect and Secretary of the (then) Vatican Congregation for Seminaries and Universities.

His last work was *'Nobility and Analogous Traditional Elites'* (1993), a masterpiece of Catholic Social doctrine on the role of natural leadership and social hierarchy in the rebuilding of an authentic Christian order. A number of Cardinals, Archbishops and Bishops acclaimed this study.

In the words of Austrian Cardinal Alfons Stickler: *"An excellent instrument of restoration of a sound natural ethics that will lead mankind to the peace, prosperity and happiness which only the authentic and genuine values are able to realize and guarantee"*.

---

[118] *Il Crociato del secolo XX:* Plinio Corrêa de Oliveira, Piemme, Casale Monferrato 1996.

Plinio Correa de Oliveira wrote many other books, articles and manifestos, as well as set in motion public campaigns in defence of Catholic Social Teaching, especially against the infiltration of Marxism in Catholic thinking and praxis through the ill-famed 'Liberation Theology.'

His fearless initiatives attracted the support of many lay and ecclesiastical personalities, as well as the wrath of a variety of others, who, having abandoned the orthodoxy of the faith, saw themselves unmasked and refuted.

Unable as they were to refute his logic and knowledge, they often appealed to the last argument of those who have no argument - 'authority' - in a vain attempt to silence his voice and stifle his pen.

Like Sir Thomas More, Plinio Correa deOliveira soldiered on regardless, unafraid of criticism and always faithful to the Magisterium of the true Church.

Plínio Correa de Oliveira went to his eternal reward in 1995. His saga lives on in the hearts and minds of lay Catholics who were fortunate enough to benefit from his teaching, guidance and paternal affection.

Saint Gabriel Communications International is proud to derive its inspiration, encouragement and enthusiasm to fight the good combat from the great Crusader of the 20th Century.

Today, a dreadful process of de-Christianisation afflicts the Western world and the sinister smoke of Satan has penetrated the Sanctuary. But we do not fear, reassured by the promise of Our Lord that the gates of hell will not prevail against His Church and in the promise made by His heavenly Mother in Fatima that *'In the end, My Immaculate Heart will Triumph!'*

We, therefore, forge ahead certain that, sooner or later, all who endeavour to imitate the fidelity to the Church shown by laymen of the calibre of Sir Thomas More and Plínio Correa de Oliveira, will proclaim the world over:

Christus vincit, Christus regnat, Christus imperat!

Raymond and Theresa de Souza
Saint Gabriel Communications International

A Vision of the Future

By Saints John Bosco and Dominic Savio

The following account refers to an event in the life of Saint Dominic Savio, the faithful disciple and spiritual son of Dom Bosco. He died in his 15th year of age, 1857, leaving behind a record of eminent sanctity. He was beatified in 1950 and canonised in 1954.

The event was related by St. John Bosco himself in his work 'Life of Dominic Savio'.

'Dominic Savio spoke frequently about the Roman Pontiff [Pius IX], expressing his great desire to see him before his own death. Several times he affirmed that he had certain things of great important to communicate to the Pontiff.

As he frequently repeated these words, one day I asked him what was it he had to tell the Pope that was so important.

'If I could speak with the Pope', Dominic said, 'I would tell him that amidst the great tribulations that await him, he should not cease to work with particular solicitude for the conversion of England. God prepares a great triumph for Catholicism in that kingdom.'

'And what makes you say that?' I asked.

'I will tell you, but I do not wish you to tell other people, as they might laugh at me. However, if you go to Rome, please tell it to Pius IX.

'One morning, while I was doing my thanksgiving after Holy Communion, I was taken by a strong distraction. It seemed that I was on a very vast flat land surface, full of people surrounded by thick darkness. They were walking, but did so as though they had lost their way and could not see where they set their feet.

Someone beside me said, 'This region is England.'

'I was going to ask other things when I saw the Supreme Pontiff, Pius IX, just as I had seen him in some pictures. He was dressed in a majestic fashion, carrying in his hands a splendorous light, and advancing amidst the multitude of people. As He advanced, the darkness gradually disappeared and the people were bathed with so much light that it seemed noon time.

'The friend said, 'This light is the Catholic Religion, which must illuminate England.'

Dom Bosco continues:

'In the year 1857, [precisely the year when St Dominic Savio died] I went to Rome and wished to tell this vision to the Supreme Pontiff, who listened to me with gentleness and contentment.

'This narration', said the Pope, 'confirms in me my determination to work without rest in favour of England, which is already the object of all my solicitudes.'

Dom Bosco concluded the narration by saying that 'I omit many other similar facts, and am content with writing them down [in other record] leaving to others the task of publishing them when they believe it will be convenient for the greater glory of God.'

(Apud *Memorie Biografiche di Don Giovanni Bosco*, compiled by Fr. Giovanni Battista Lemoyne S.D.B.; and in part the Spanish version of Fr. Rodolfo Fierro S.D.B., published in *Biografía y escritos de San Juan Bosco*, BAC, Madri, 1955).

Saint Dominic Savio had that vision in the year of his death, 1857, precisely 150 years ago. In the sesquicentennial anniversary of that encouraging vision of the future, we hope and pray that the current movement among Anglicans to come home to Rome be blessed by God with superabundant fruits, so that, the vision of St. Dominic being fulfilled, a Counter-Revolution aimed to reconquer Europe and the West for Christ the King may be triggered, for the greater glory of God, salvation of souls and prosperity for England and all Christian nations.

Perhaps it might not be out of place to mention what the Blessed Virgin Mary said to Maximin (one of the seers) in Her apparition at La Salette, France, in 1846, merely four years prior to the Emancipation of the Catholic Hierarchy in England:

"A Protestant nation in the north shall be converted to the Faith, and through the means of that nation, the others shall return to the Holy Catholic Church".

What a great moment in History it would be, if, or hopefully *when*, four and a half centuries after *the Island of the Saints* severed ties with the Sacraments that its Royal *Defender of the Faith* affirmed in so stern a manner, sons and daughters of England were to reaffirm them, and bring *Our Lady's Dowry* back home to Rome.

England would enter History as the usher of authentic Christian unity in Europe, *en route* to that revitalisation of Christendom to resist the inroads of the enemies of the Cross of Christ in the Old continent.

God's will be done.

SAINT GABRIEL COMMUNICATIONS INTERNATIONAL

Founded in 1998 in the Archdiocese of Perth, Western Australia, *Saint Gabriel Communications* is today Australia's leading international outreach promoting Catholic Apologetics.

The Lay Apologist Raymond de Souza, its founder and director, is today the host of three 13-episode program series at the *Eternal Word Television Network* (EWTN), the largest Catholic television in the planet. He is also the Program Director for Portuguese-speaking countries for *Human Life International*, Chairman of the *Sacred Heart Legion* and Member of the Advisory Board of *Catholics Come Home Inc.*

Brazilian by birth, Catholic by grace, Australian by choice.

In the last quarter century Raymond has distinguished himself as international lay Catholic Apologist – broadcaster – Pro-Life activist – Catholic Action militant, addressing audiences in five continents to *"re-evangelise the baptised"*, as Pope John Paul II exhorted the faithful laity to do in *"Crossing the Threshold of Hope"*.

Over the years, Raymond has given more than 3,500 talks on Catholic apologetics and related topics, in person, on radio and television, putting *Logic at the service of the Faith*, blending wit, history and humour in a unique and riveting style.

His work has assisted religious education and pro-life programs at parishes, schools, and lay organizations in Brazil, Canada, the United

States, South Africa, New Zealand, Fiji, Australia, Singapore, England, Wales, Scotland, Ireland, Austria and Portugal.

More recently, he has also addressed Catholic audiences in Italy, Poland, Belgium, Luxembourg, Tanzania, Mozambique, Cape Verde Islands, East Timor, Peru and the Philippines.

From its original office at the Cathedral Parish Centre in the Archdiocese of Perth, Western Australia, and now headquartered in Sydney, *Saint Gabriel Communications* expanded its work of Catholic Apologetics throughout Australia. Its highly acclaimed educational program *New Apologetics by Mail* reaches Catholics in all Australian states.

Radio and Television

Over the years in both New Zealand and Australia Raymond has hosted various broadcasts.

"Crossroads Challenge" was his first radio show, produced in cooperation with the *Alternative Ministry of the Auckland diocese*. His second show was *"Mission: Possible!"* produced in the Christchurch Diocese with the support of the Most Reverend Basil Meeking, his diocesan bishop. *"Sounds Catholic"* in Western Australia was sponsored by the Most Rev. Barry Hickey, Archbishop of Perth. In his section, *"Radio Replies,"* Raymond answered write-in questions on faith and morals.

The success of that program led to a live call-in talk show called *"The Layman's Hour"* which he produced with his wife, Theresa.

Every Sunday evening for two years, Raymond and Theresa enlivened the airwaves with news, interviews, reports and animated exchanges with callers.

Today, Raymond's work has been featured on EWTN global Catholic network. His first series, *"Good or Evil: Who Decides?"* reaches millions of homes worldwide via satellite, cable and internet.

His second series, *"Jesus Christ, true God and True man"*, masterly defends the divinity of Jesus in the face of the growth of secularism, agnosticism and Islam.

His third series on the 'Twelve Promises of the Sacred Heart' investigates the each one of Jesus' promises to those who are faithful to His Sacred Heart, and the benefits received by them.

Catholic Action and pro-Life work

Throughout his career, Raymond has been involved in numerous Catholic lay movements. These include *Young Canadians for a Christian Civilisation* (Montreal); *Young South Africans for a Christian Civilisation* (Johannesburg); and *New Zealand Family Action* (Wellington).

In Australia, he founded and directs the *Legion of Saint Gabriel* (training of laity to defend the Faith) and the *Marian Eucharistic Alliance* (rediscovery of the sense of the sacred in Catholic liturgy and spirituality).

He also founded the Cathedral branch of the *Catholic Order of the Knights of the Southern Cross* in Perth and was Coordinator of Lay Associate members of the *Australian Confraternity of Catholic Clergy* in Western Australia.

Raymond's extensive pro-life work is highlighted by his assistance of South African pro-life hero, Dr. Claude Newbury, within the ranks of *Human Life International*.

In New Zealand, he was a member of the national board of the *Coalition of Concerned Citizens* and president of the most active branch of the *Society for the Protection of the Unborn Child*.

In Perth, Australia, he was the coordinator of *Human Life International*.

In 2002, the London-based *International Alliance of Catholic Knights* awarded Raymond the prestigious International 'Michael Bell' Award for *'Initiatives for Life,'* in acknowledgement of his long series of pro-life initiatives.

Languages

Gifted in the use of languages, Raymond worked in New Zealand as translator, interpreter and tutor of Portuguese, Spanish, French, Italian and English.

His clients included the *New Zealand Ministry of Internal Affairs*; *Victoria University Centre for Continuing Education*, the *Wellington Community Institute* and the *New Zealand Translators*.

He also provided intensive language training in Spanish to members of New Zealand's diplomatic corps in Latin American countries, some of whom were subsequently commissioned to Spain and the Holy See.

Within the ranks of today's Catholic Apologists, there are some who defend the Faith in more than one language.

Raymond defends it in four.

Although English is the first language of his apostolate, he also addresses audiences in French, Spanish, and Portuguese (his native language) upon request.

The Sacred Heart Legion

In the United States, Raymond promotes devotion to the Sacred Heart of Jesus as a vital means of sanctification for Catholic Action. He is assisted in this important work by his wife, Theresa, and his teenage children.

Together, they have set in motion the *Sacred Heart Legion* as a primary means to re-evangelize the baptized.

The Legion' mission is fourfold:

(1) *To revive the notions of good and evil* to combat the loss of the sense of sin and virtue.

(2) *To defend the Divinity of Jesus Christ* as a response to the de-Christianisation of the West caused by secularism, agnosticism and Islam;

(3) *To defend the Real Presence of Jesus in the Eucharist* to 're-evangelise the baptized' and

(4) To promote the knowledge, love and service of the Sacred Heart of Jesus through the twelve promises and the True Devotion of the Sacred Heart. The special website www.SacredHeartLegion.com invites Catholics the world over to say *'yes!'* to the Sacred Heart and thus work to recall the promises, rekindle the fervour and reconquer the nation to His Kingship.

In his masterpiece *'Revolution and Counter-Revolution'*, Professor Plínio Corrêa de Oliveira echoes the Pontifical Magisterium and underlines the need to revive the notions of good and evil as an indispensable requirement of any Catholic Action worthy of this name, and which aims to restore Christian Civilization according to the Mind of the Church.

The *New Apologetics of Faith and Reason* promoted by Raymond de Souza via *St Gabriel Communications* aims precisely to put this teaching into practice.

Please visit the site www.RaymonddeSouza.com and click on the link titled 'Catalog' for a variety of CD's, EWTN DVD's and books on Catholic apologetics.

For a list of topics addressed by Raymond de Souza, please visit us online and select 'Booking', or contact www.parousiamedia.com for CD and DVD titles and more information.

www.parousiamedia.com

Other Recommended sites:

www.KeysofPeter.org

www.SacredHeartLegion.com